Love Poems

Love Poems

Alexander Pushkin

Edited and translated by Roger Clarke

With translations by

James Falen, Jill Higgs, R.H. Morrison, John Coutts,
Mary Hobson, David and Lyudmila Matthews,
Walter Arndt, Walter Morison, B. Kelley

ALMA CLASSICS

ALMA CLASSICS LTD
London House
243–253 Lower Mortlake Road
Richmond
Surrey TW9 2LL
United Kingdom
www.almaclassics.com

Love Poems first published by Alma Classics Ltd in 2013
This revised edition published by Alma Classics Ltd in 2014

Printed in Great Britain by CPI Group (UK) Ltd, Croydon CR0 4YY

Typeset by Tetragon, London

ISBN: 978-1-84749-300-2

Contents

Alexander Pushkin (1799–1837)

Introduction

Pushkin's poetry is remarkable in many ways. It is remarkable for its quantity: quite apart from his narrative and dramatic verse, he has well over seven hundred shorter poems (including unpublished drafts and unfinished fragments) to his name. It is remarkable for the period it spans, stretching from his early schooldays to his premature death at the age of thirty-seven. It is remarkable for its range: it extends from deeply felt expressions of love and friendship, joy and pain, through acute and sensitive reflections on life, polished and entertaining society verse, to jokes, invectives and epigrams; it includes verse epistles, ballads, stories, descriptive pieces and songs; it covers, as well as personal and social matters, political, historical, philosophical and religious subjects; and it embraces not only purely original work but adaptations, imitations and parodies, not only of Russian literature and folklore but also of poetry from the Greco-Roman world, from modern Europe, and even from the Orient.

Pushkin himself was a remarkable man. Not only could he write poetry of technical excellence, he was also intelligent, independent, sensitive and penetratingly observant. Though he could be proud, self-pitying, angry and harshly critical, he also knew the importance of sincerity, loyalty and forgiveness. He had other weaknesses: he was an inveterate gambler and womanizer and could sometimes be excitable and petty; but he was also capable of generosity, of human understanding, and of establishing deep and lasting relationships. Another redeeming feature was his irrepressible sense of humour: to a much greater extent than most writers, he prized what was "light and cheerful". These qualities shine through in his writing; in particular, in his concision, clarity, directness, honesty and pervasive irony. One rarely goes away from reading Pushkin depressed – rather, stimulated, enlightened and exhilarated.

This goes to explain the singularity of Pushkin. There were other talented poets and writers among his immediate predecessors and contemporaries who displayed some of his characteristics, but his was a uniquely full and attractive combination. That is why he holds such an eminent place in Russian – indeed in European – literature.

The scope of this volume, however, is limited to Pushkin's love poetry – though it is astonishing how even the love poems span most of the forms mentioned in the first paragraph. Of Pushkin's total output of short poems his love poetry accounts for only perhaps a quarter. Even within this group we have had to be selective, and so have omitted insubstantial fragments and poems that, while meaningful to Pushkin's contemporaries, are now difficult to appreciate without an extensive explanation of references and background. In total we have chosen 113 love poems, ranging across the spectrum of love's orientations and expressions, from the imaginatively fictional to the starkly real, from playful society *bons mots* to heartfelt expressions of deepest feeling.

The poems are arranged broadly in chronological order of composition, so far as is practicable and can be ascertained. Of course, the main point of a book such as this is to allow the poems to be enjoyed for themselves. But as many of the poems are autobiographical, we wanted the volume to tell a story: the story of Pushkin's personal and social life and his emotional development, as seen through his love affairs, real and imagined, from ebullient boyhood, through impetuous youth and more measured maturity, into the regrets and frustrations of middle age. To provide a framework for this storytelling, the poems are grouped into six parts representing the major periods of his life.

In reading the poems as autobiography, one must bear in mind the limitations of this approach. Although Pushkin's autographs, notebooks and correspondence allow scholars to date many of his poems quite accurately, in other cases dating is conjectural. Also, for understandable reasons, it was rare for Pushkin to name the addressees of his love poems; indeed he often did his best to disguise them behind pseudonyms or anonymity. Identification of the unnamed women he mentions is a complex and precarious field of study that has to draw not only on reading a poem's often enigmatic contents, but on scrutinizing Pushkin's rough drafts, deciphering other references in his notebooks and correspondence, and eavesdropping on the not always reliable comments and reminiscences of contemporaries.

Some of Pushkin's love poetry, particularly in the early years, did not relate to real people at all, but was the construct of his literary interests and imagination. Even when a real woman was the original inspiration for a poem, the facts may have evolved into something more abstract by the time Pushkin came to writing it down. It is worth quoting Pushkin's own account (albeit as the semi-autobiographical narrator of the fictional *Eugene Onegin*) of how he went about writing romantic verses:

> ...every poet enjoys dreaming of love. Time was when objects of affection used to appear to me in dreams: I kept their image concealed within my heart, and afterwards my verse brought them to life...
>
> These days my friends quite often ask me: "Whom are these amorous verses of yours about? All of the girls are jealous – say who's the dedicatee of this one? Whose glance stirred your imagination and won you, for your wistful lyrics, an affectionate caress? Who have your lines immortalized?"

My word of honour, friends: it's none of them. I've not found any relief at all for love's dementing anguish. Lucky's the man who's managed to combine with a love affair the fever of composition! He's followed Petrarch's footsteps: he'll not only have doubled poetry's sacred ecstasy, but he'll have soothed his inner pain as well – *and* gained himself a reputation!

But I've been always dull and mute in love. Not till love's passed does inspiration come and clear the darkness from my mind; then, free at last, I once more seek to unite my feelings and thoughts with the magic of words. I write; my heart has ceased to ache; my pen no longer absent-mindedly clutters the margin of unfinished lines with drawings of women's heads or dainty feet. The extinguished embers will flare up no more. I *am* still sad; but there are no more tears; and soon in the wake of the storm, yes very soon, deep calm will settle on my soul. And then I'll begin to write…

(*Eugene Onegin* I, 57–59, translated by Roger Clarke)

So the extraction of pure autobiographical fact from a thick overlay of subjective memory and creative inspiration is not an easy process, and will always remain largely a matter of deduction, intuition and conjecture.

The chronological arrangement of the poems also allows us to follow Pushkin's literary development over the same period. But a word of warning here too: in the sixth section of this collection, representing Pushkin's final years after marriage, there is a sharp decline in the quantity and emotional intensity of the love poetry. It would be a great mistake to interpret this decline as evidencing a decline in the quantity or quality of Pushkin's writing more generally. It is hardly surprising that a poet's output of love poetry should dwindle after marriage, particularly when, as in Pushkin's case, the marriage begins successfully and the poet is determined to resist extramarital affairs. In fact the early 1830s were years when Pushkin focused more on prose writing; but he continued even then to produce fine lyric poetry on historical, literary, philosophical and religious themes.

To help fit the poems, whether autobiographical or not, into the framework of Pushkin's life, a short biography of Pushkin is provided at the back of this volume.

Between the poems and the biography there is a brief commentary on each poem, supplying what information is available about the dates of composition and publication, if published during Pushkin's lifetime. Many of the poems were only recovered after his death from his notebooks, or in a few cases from the records or recollections of friends. There could be several reasons for Pushkin not publishing them himself: he may have considered them – some of the album verses, for example – too slight and ephemeral; some may have been too personal, to himself or to others, to be published without embarrassment; he may have anticipated an adverse reaction from the censor or from the public; or he may not have had time to complete them to his satisfaction. The commentary also sets out to identify addressees (where possible), to explain obscure references, and to give the poems any relevant context or background that may interest the reader.

– Roger Clarke

Acknowledgements

I am indebted to Professor James Falen, John Coutts, Mary Hobson and David and Lyudmila Matthews for their cheerful help in preparing their admirable translations for inclusion in this book.

I am grateful to Simon Blundell, Librarian of the Reform Club, who has helped me identify and recover the texts of some of the obscure French verses referred to by Pushkin.

I also pay tribute to the memory of the late Iain Sproat, owner of Milner and Company, whose initiative in assembling and publishing for the first time English versions of all Pushkin's lyrics laid the foundation for the present volume.

I am also deeply grateful to Alessandro Gallenzi for entrusting me with the task of editing this volume, work that has given me enormous interest and enjoyment.

Finally, I am immeasurably grateful to my wife Elizabeth, who has supported me throughout in this work by providing me generously with time, encouragement and practical assistance.

Love Poems

I

1813–17

The Imperial Lycée

Reason and Love

Young Daphnis, chasing Chloë, cried:
"My beauty, wait! Don't run away!
Just say: I love you – please don't hide;
I swear by Venus, I won't stay!"
"Keep silent!" Reason coldly said.
"Now say: 'I like you'!" Eros pled.

"I like you!" sang the maiden sweet,
and love set both their hearts ablaze,
and Daphnis fell before her feet,
and Chloë dropped her flaming gaze.
"Oh flee! Oh flee!" cold Reason cried,
while crafty Eros "Stay!" replied.

She stayed. And, trembling with his love,
the happy shepherd made his plea:
"Oh look," he said, "that downy dove
has kissed his mate beneath the tree!"
"Oh flee!" cried Reason once again;
"They'll teach you how!" said Eros then.

And then a smile so tender spilled
across the blushing maiden's lips,
and as her eyes with languor filled,
within her lover's arms she slipped.
"Be happy!" Eros softly said.
And Reason's words? Oh, Reason fled.

translated by James Falen

The Tear

Last night behind a jug of stout
   I sat with a hussar;
and, grimly mute, I stared along
   the road, away off far.

My comrade asked: "Why, tell me, does
   the highway hold your gaze?
You've yet to see your mates march off
   along it, God be praised!"

Dejectedly I hung my head
   and whispered in reply:
"Friend, she's deserted me!...", and then
   fell silent with a sigh.

A tear rolled glistening from my eye
   and dropped into the stout.
"What, cry about a girl, young lad!
   Oh shame!" my friend burst out.

"Leave off, hussar!... My heart – it aches!
   No pain's touched *you*, that's clear.
It only takes one tear, alas!
   to spoil a jug of beer!"

translated by Roger Clarke

For the Lovely Girl Who Took Snuff

Can it be so? It once was roses, Cupid's flowers,
  you loved, or a corsage of stately tulips,
    or fragrant freesias, jasmines, lilies –
you used to love them all and wear them every day
  against the marble whiteness of your breast.
    How can it be, my dear Kliména,
that you have changed your taste so inexplicably?…
      Now what you like to smell
      is not a flower, morning-fresh,
        but a green toxic weed
        that human industry's
      transformed into a powdery dust.

    That greying German academic,
      hunched in his professorial chair,
his learnèd mind immersed in Latin books –
he, as he coughs and coughs, may use his shrivelled hand
  to poke the crushed tobacco up his nose.

    That young moustachioed dragoon,
  while sitting by his window of a morning,
      still drowsy from a hangover,
  may puff grey smoke from out his meerschaum pipe.

    That erstwhile beauty in her sixties,
her charms by now retired, her love life terminated,
whose glamour's now maintained by artifice alone,
    upon whose body nowhere's left unwrinkled –
      she, as she slanders, prays and yawns,
may sniff tobacco dust, sure antidote to sorrow.

But you, my lovely one!… Yet if tobacco
so takes your fancy now – oh, blaze of inspiration! –
   yes, I could be transmuted into dust,
      incarcerated in a snuffbox,
I could be caught up on your gentle fingers;
then it would be my sweetest pleasure
to have you sprinkle me upon your breast
beneath your silken hanky – and perhaps
even – No, empty dream! That cannot be.
   Why can't harsh Fate relent enough
      to let me be a pinch of snuff?

translated by Roger Clarke

To a Young Widow

Lída, loyal friend, my treasure,
why, as I drift off to sleep
tired but happy from our pleasure,
do I hear you softly weep?
Why, too, burning with desire,
savouring love's ecstasy,
do I on your cheek descry a
tear you tried to hide from me?
When I speak, you disregard me,
deaf to love that I express;
cold your gaze when you regard me,
cold your hand when mine you press.
Dearest friend beyond all value,
tears for ever shall you shed?
Futilely for ever shall you
call your spouse back from the dead?
Death-sleep's chilly grip, uneasing,
holds its victims fast: believe!
Pleasant voice to them's not pleasing,
sighs of grief won't make them grieve.
Unaware are they of gravestones
strewn with roses, radiant skies,
noisy wakes, the tears of loved ones,
and a girlfriend's choked goodbyes.
Yes, the friend you still remember
breathed his last – too soon! One night
he began his final slumber,
nestling by you in delight.
He now rests in blest contentment.
Wrong to love are we, then? No!
None will rise up in resentment
from the timeless dark below;

thunderclaps won't crash above us;
nor will any phantom creep,
vengeful, up on us young lovers,
startling us too soon from sleep.

translated by Roger Clarke

To Elvína

Elvína, come, give me your hand, dear heart;
cut short this heavy dream that wearies me.
Speak… Will I see… Or must we stay apart,
    condemned by destiny?

Shall there be no more meetings face to face?
Must all my days be veiled in constant night?
Shall we no more be caught in love's embrace
    by a new morning's light?

Elvína, as the night's dark hours fly by,
may I not hold you tight, my blood on fire,
gaze at you, dear, with languid, longing eye
    and tremble with desire –

and then, in joy beyond all speech or measure,
listen to your sweet lisp, your gentle cry,
and drowse through pleasing night to waking pleasure,
    just we two, you and I?

translated by Roger Clarke

The Moon

Out of the clouds why do you venture,
oh solitary moon, and on
the pillow where I lie alone
squander your melancholy splendour?
You with your gloomy visitation
awaken dreams of love, the pain
of hopeless passion, and the vain
longings of lovers' aspiration
that reason hardly can allay.
Sad recollections, fly away!
Sleep, love that failed us both outright!
There'll never come again that night,
when, moon, with your mysterious ray
of placid radiance, you shone
through heavy curtains on my bed,
and gentle, gentle lustre shed
upon my sweetheart's lovely form.
Why, precious moments, did you press
with such a haste to fly away,
and shadows pale to nothingness,
extinguished by unwelcome day?
How was it, moon, your lustre fell
away in bright dawn's radiance?
Why did the morning light advance?
Why did I bid my love farewell?

translated by Jill Higgs and Roger Clarke

To Morpheus

O Morpheus, god of dreams, till day
grant me relief from love's distress.
Come, blow my lamp out now, I pray,
and my nocturnal visions bless!
Block from my cheerless recollection
the dreadful pain of those goodbyes;
grant me to see her loving eyes,
and hear her murmurs of affection.
Then, once the dark has taken flight,
your power over vision ended,
oh how I wish my poor wits might
forget love till fresh night's descended!

translated by Roger Clarke

For Friends

On you, my friends, the gods above
still lavish golden nights and days:
on you is fixed, with thought of love,
every young girl's attentive gaze.
Play on then, comrades, for the while;
sing out your songs and raise your glasses;
and, as the transient evening passes,
through tears on your brief joys I'll smile.

translated by R.H. Morrison and Roger Clarke

The Singer

Did you not hear, among the trees by night,
the one who of his love and loss was singing?
And when the fields lay silent in the morning,
a pipe's soft sound, so sorrowful, so slight,
   did you not hear?

Did you not meet, in lonely forest glades,
the one who of his love and loss was singing? –
not see the stain of tears, nor mark him smiling?
His gentle glance, his melancholy gaze,
   did you not meet?

Did you not sigh to hear his quiet voice –
the one who of his love and loss was singing?
When in the woods you met the young lad drifting,
and caught the eye that could no more rejoice,
   did you not sigh?

translated by Roger Clarke

Cupid and Hymen

Listen, husbands – pay attention:
funnier tale is hard to find...
Here's the story... Dare I mention
Cupid? He's the god who's blind –
wears a scarf around his eyes?
Stop! I fear your poet lies.
Cupid sees too well – bad lad!
Likes to drive us mortals mad.
Making mischief – I'm afraid –
seems to be his stock in trade...
Long ago – and who knows why? –
saucy Cupid thought he'd try
another ploy – a new surprise;
doffed the scarf that bound his eyes,
chuckled, paused... and went to see
Hymen... Who could Hymen be?
Vulcan's grumpy elder son,
cold and lazy – that's the one! –
dull, decrepit, frankly boring,
– every age endures his snoring –
jealous... Jealousy... dear me!
That's the vice that stops him sleeping,
makes him wake to play the sentry,
hold the tiresome torch up high,
prowl and peep and pry and spy,
– everlasting lookout keeping –
just to block his brother's entry...
Now my godling dares a greeting:
"Every quarrel has its end!
Journeys end in brothers meeting:
worthy Hymen, be my friend!
How absurd this long and truceless

quarrel – how entirely useless!
Let's be wise and let's be clever:
here's my blindfold – yours for ever!
I'll accept your torch, my dear…
just a little souvenir…"
Gloomy Hymen – can you guess? –
mutters a reluctant "yes"…
Cupid simply jumps for joy!
There and then the saucy boy
ties that blindfold o-so-tight:
binds it on with all his might!
Why – since then – should Beauty dread
base intrusive observation?
Hymen's dull perambulation
quite neglects the nuptial bed.
Cupid never seems to pause;
dares to wage a truly shocking
war against his brother's cause
(matrimonial honour mocking)!
Let's reveal what darkness covers:
after husbands fall asleep
see the cunning Cupid creep,
hand the torch to happy lovers,
warm the bed of bliss – and keep
laughing watch… The tale's concluded…
Is the moral plain and clear?
Dreary Hymen well excluded?
Take my meaning, Helen dear…

translated by John Coutts

A Window

Not long ago I rode one evening
along a misty path for home,
and by the moonlight dimly gleaming
I saw a lass who sat alone
inside a window, where, reflecting,
she seemed by vague forebodings filled,
and restlessly she kept inspecting
the shadowed path that skirts the hills.

"I'm here!" there came a breathless murmur.
She, deftly as her fears allowed,
unlatched the window with a tremor...
The moon then passed behind a cloud.
"You lucky man!" I muttered, grieving.
"A jolly night's in store for you.
How long to wait before, one evening,
for me a window opens too?"

translated by Roger Clarke

Her

"What's up with you? Be honest. Why this gloom?"
"Friend, I'm in love!" "With whom? Come on, reveal her."
"With *her*." "But who? Glitséra, Chloë, Lila?"
"Not them." "You worship someone, though – say whom?"
"*Her, her*, that's whom!" "My friend, you're being rather
coy and offhand! How is it you can be
so tetchy? Who's at fault? Her husband? father?…"
"No, no, friend!" "Well?" "To *her* I'm never *he*."

translated by Roger Clarke

Notice on the Infirmary Wall

Look, here's a student lying ill;
he'll not recover, that's for sure.
Don't try to dose him with a pill:
love's sickness is beyond a cure!

translated by Roger Clarke

For Delivery to the Bábolovsky Palace

You loveliest of all! May Russia's demigod
enjoy here in your arms an ecstasy complete.
   How highly Fortune's favoured you!
At his feet lies the world – here he lies at your feet.

translated by Roger Clarke

II

1817–20

St Petersburg

Friendship and Love

Friendship alone, I've heard it said,
makes our world beautiful. Without it
there is no joy. The path we tread
would be too hard, no doubt about it,
but for quiet friendship's light ahead.
But listen – there's another feeling:
it both caresses and torments;
in times of struggle, times of healing,
its flame is equally intense;
it's cruel and excruciating,
it numbs our souls which, scarce alive
with wounds profound and devastating,
the balm of hope cannot revive...
This is the passion I've endured!...
I languish, perish in my prime,
but God forbid I should be cured...

translated by Mary Hobson

Yours and Mine

"Yours and mine –" said Lafontaine,
"these words caused the world's decline!"
That opinion isn't mine.
What's your view, my dear Clymène?
If you were no longer mine,
and I no more yours – what then?

translated by Roger Clarke

Ye Gods!

Ye gods, how danger mingles with delight!
I hear your voice… gaze at your tender face…
enjoy your smiling glance – alluring sight! –
your words that spellbind with their fire and grace!
Enchantress, say: what magic drew me here?
Through meeting you, I've caught a glimpse of bliss –
and come to hate all that I'd held most dear.

translated by John Coutts

To Yelizavéta Ogaryóva,

to whom the bishop sent some fruit from his garden.

Sending you fruit from his domain,
the bishop – shameless show-off he! –
meant to present himself – that's plain –
as procreation's deity.

Nothing's beyond you – smiling grace
will win senility with ease;
you'll set the bishop's heart ablaze
and bring him senseless to your knees.

Now he has met your magic gaze,
the cross he wears he'll quite forget,
and he'll sing tender hymns of praise
to your divine charms, Lisabet.

translated by Roger Clarke

My Homeland

Lover of unfamiliar foreign lands,
and constant critic of my land of birth,
I often said: "Where can we find at home
true intellect and genius of worth?
Where's there a citizen of noble soul,
a lofty spirit, longing to be free?
Where's there a woman, not of frigid beauty,
but charm that burns with real vitality?
Where can I find spontaneous conversation,
enlightened, full of sparkling words that shine?
With whom can one be warm, not cold and empty?"
I'd almost come to hate this land of mine.
But yesterday Golítsyna just smiled,
and to my homeland I was reconciled.

translated by David and Lyudmila Matthews

For Princess Golítsyna

on sending her the ode "Freedom"

As Nature's simple devotee,
I'd written this to celebrate
freedom as a sublime ideal;
I'd be its sweet-tongued advocate.
Now seeing, hearing you, I waver;
I yield, more feebly than I should.
Since liberty I've lost for good,
it's now captivity I favour.

translated by Roger Clarke

Madrigal for M—

All you whom love has never fired with yearning,
just glance at her, and love will blaze in you.
All you who've loved, but felt life's chill returning,
just glance at her – you'll blaze with love anew.

translated by Roger Clarke

To A. B—

What can we quickly say in verse to greet her?
    To tell the truth's my only aim.
Unthinking, I shall say: "There's no one sweeter";
    and, having thought, I'll say the same.

translated by Roger Clarke

For Catherine Bakúnina

To mark your name day well I've tried – but there's no way,
for all the zeal with which I worship at your feet.
No sweeter are you now upon St Catherine's day,
because on any day you couldn't be more sweet.

translated by Roger Clarke

To Shcherbínin

The man's a lucky one, dear friend,
who's never plagued by fools' emotions,
who lacks the time to fall in love,
who's always active, always cheerful;
who of an evening strokes his floozy
over a strictly private dinner,
washing down richest Strasbourg pâté
with red wine of the best bouquet;
who, having banished all distractions,
will spend a night of pure devotion –
true devotee of Aphrodite –
with Love's young priestess at his side.
He's drowsing happily next morning,
while leafing through his pet review.
All day's devoted to amusement;
by night, though, Love's again supreme.

You randy playboy friend Shcherbínin,
don't *we* spend our time too like this,
making the most of youth and health
with love and fun-making and wine?
But our young lives will fly away;
the time for love and fun will go.
Then we'll be numb to strong emotion,
our hearts will shrivel up and freeze.
There'll be no girlfriends then, no singing,
no more intense desires, no joys –
all the relief we'll find, dear friend,
is in those "mists of reminiscence".
At death's dark door I'll shake my head
and say regretfully to you,
"Dear chap, do you recall Annette?"
then we'll just smile a smile, we two.

translated by Roger Clarke

For Olga Masson

Olga, Aphrodite's nursling,
Olga, paragon of love,
you're so expert at disbursing
both caresses and rebuffs!
Only one voluptuous kiss
was enough to stir our heart,
and an hour of magic bliss
we believed you'd set apart.
Up we ran with lovers' speed
at the time that you'd agreed,
dealt your door a hundredth blow,
heard your surreptitious mumbling
and the sleepy housemaid's grumbling,
then your last derisive "No".

In the name of lovers' licence,
and of money and of calm,
of Priapic self-indulgence
and your tantalizing charm,
hear our love-crazed lamentation,
Olga, priestess of delight:
we crave rapture and elation –
don't refuse us: name the night.

translated by Roger Clarke

That's when She'll Come…

That's when she'll come to join me – late,
when all the world's retired to slumber,
the time all good things lie recumbent
and all bad things are standing straight.

translated by Roger Clarke

Recovery

My dear friend, was it you I saw?
Or was it just a ghost, a mirage in the heat,
a vague and muddled dream born of my malady,
that came to rouse my fevered fancy with deceit?
And in the darkest hour of my life-threatening illness
did you, a gentle girl, stand there above my bed,
clad like a horse guardsman with charming awkwardness?
I saw you dimly, yes: my eyes, though clouded, read
charms that I recognized beneath that battle dress;
and, feebly whispering, I named the girl I knew...
Those dark imaginings, though, once more filled my mind;
And in the gloom my hand, though feeble, groped for you.
Then all at once I felt your breath, your gentle tears,
a moist kiss on my brow that fever had made to smart;
   it stirred – ye gods! – such violent desire,
rekindling into flame life's fire to warm my heart!
   My blood boiled up, my body shook...
   And then you vanished – temptress! – like a ghost.
A cruel friend you are! This ecstasy exhausts me.
   Oh come! Love's killing me almost.
   Be kind, and in the silent night
appear, you sorceress, and once more let me see
beneath that fearsome helmet your celestial eyes,
   your cloak, your belt, your livery,
your legs so fetching in their knee-boots, battle-ready.
Seductive warrior! Quick, hurry, I implore!
I'm waiting for you; come! The gods have granted me
   their blessed gift of health once more,
   and, with it, sweet anxiety
to share some youthful mischief and love's mystery.

translated by Roger Clarke

Doráda – and Another

Doráda cheers my heart… I love her golden hair,
the light-blue eyes she has, her pale and languid air…
Abandoning my friends, I left the feast last night
and tasted in her arms the fullness of delight;
fresh ecstasies replaced each ecstasy that dwindled,
and passions quickly slaked were once again rekindled;
I swooned, but in the dim uncertainty of night
another's lovely form intruded on my sight,
and, stricken with a sad and secret sense of shame,
I heard my lips call out an unexpected name.

translated by James Falen

Trustful Love – for Dorída

Yes, I believe I'm loved; and this belief relieves me.
It's inconceivable my darling would deceive me;
in her there's no pretence: her passion's unforced glow,
her bashfulness – best gift the Graces can bestow –
the charming nonchalance of how she speaks and dresses,
and all those playful names her childlike love expresses.

translated by Roger Clarke

Platonic Love

Lida, my sweet young friend, I know
the one to whom you've dedicated
those hours you spend in fond reflection,
the one you serve in silent worship,
unseen by girlfriends' prying eyes.
You're scared, though, of that mischief-maker,
the charming little wingèd boy-god;
nor can you face his brother Hymen
with that one's frigid gravity.
Obedient to your disposition,
it's quite another god you pray to.
Yes, tender feelings meant for you
have found their path a barren one.
I recognize that look of yours –
the feebly glowing, half-closed eyes,
the pallid, never-blushing cheeks,
the listless, languid way you walk...
That god of yours will never grant
his worshippers a joy that's full.
Girls that are innocent rate highly
the private benefits he offers:
he's partial to romantic dreaming,
he's not put off by locks on doors,
he favours modest, chaste enjoyments –
Love's brother too, but he's a loner.
Whenever, Lida, late at night
you lie dissatisfied and sleepless,
he brings mysteriously to life
the troubled thoughts that haunt your mind;
your every sigh, poor girl, he echoes,
dispelling in his quiet way
not only dreams of adult love,

but the calm chastity you prized.
You think that you'll escape from Love
in pleasures you enjoy alone.
No hope of that! Those very pleasures
will but revive your deep unease.

Will Eros never see the precinct
destined for him, but not yet hallowed?
Your beauty, like a rose, is fading;
your youth's brief moments race away.
Surely my prayer won't go unanswered?
Bid your misguided dreams adieu –
your loveliness won't last for ever;
you're lovely – but not just for you!

translated by Roger Clarke

In Sosnítskaya's Album

You've managed to combine your magic eyes' allure –
   their charm, their fire – with heart completely cold.
   Whoever loves you is a fool for sure;
but he who loves you not is fool a hundredfold.

translated by Roger Clarke

Aimed at Kólosova

Kólosova's great as Esther –
movingly enunciating,
regally perambulating,
long dark tresses, purple vesture,
tender voice and loving eye,
hands smeared white as any sheet,
eyebrows black with charcoal dye,
and those quite enormous feet!

translated by Roger Clarke

For Katénin

Her charming face I long to see –
will someone send me, please, her picture?
Till banished, I adored the theatre
and was her vocal devotee.
But, when she appeared, her radiant beauty
wreathed icon-like in incense smoke,
carping maybe beyond my duty,
I spoilt her plaudits with a joke.
I curse the injustice that I've done,
I curse that jibe (what could be meaner?),
refuted by the acclaim she's won
as Célimène and as Moïna!
You deities of dramatic art,
this imbecile's caused you vexation;
he'll soon though, with a contrite heart,
bring you new gifts in expiation.

translated by Roger Clarke

Song of the Twelve Girls

from Ruslan and Lyudmila *(Fourth Canto)*

The moors grow dim at eventide;
chill air blows off the Dnieper's waters;
come, traveller-boy, it's late to ride;
take shelter in our homely quarters.

By night there's rest and comfort here;
by day loud feasting fills our hall.
We'll welcome you: come at our call;
come, traveller-boy, we're waiting here.

You'll find a throng of beauties here,
who'll coax and kiss you, charmers all.
We'll tell no tales: come at our call;
come, traveller-boy, we're waiting here.

When day dawns and you go from here,
we'll fill your cup to toast us all.
We mean no harm: come at our call;
come, traveller boy, we're waiting here.

The moors grow dim at eventide;
chill air blows off the Dnieper's waters;
come, traveller-boy, it's late to ride;
take shelter in our homely quarters.

translated by Roger Clarke

III

1820–24

In the South

Epilogue to *Ruslan and Lyudmila*

So – carefree, cosmopolitan,
at ease, at leisure, and at peace,
there was I glibly celebrating
the sombre legends of our past.
Engrossed in verse, I paid no heed to
the spite of blind ill luck and foes,
the bad faith of a false Dorída,
and the shrill chattering of fools.
Borne up on wings of fantasy,
my mind soared off beyond this earth,
while meantime thunderclouds, unnoticed,
were massing thickly overhead!...
I would have perished... But, friends, bless you,
you rescued me in those first days
just as the tempest broke; your kindness
brought me relief in my distress.
By your appeals the storm was stilled;
you gave me back my peace of mind;
saved me my freedom – precious icon
to an impetuous lad like me!
Now, far from the Nevá's embankments,
dismissed from salon talk and minds,
I'm standing awestruck – there before me
the soaring peaks of Caucasus.
High on their dizzying precipices,
where rocky gorges yawn below,
I'm drawing sustenance from feelings
I can't express, and from the breathless
beauty of vistas wild and harsh.
Within me, hour by hour, as ever,
I'm tantalized by thoughts aplenty –
but my poetic fire is spent.

I seek in vain for stimulation:
passed is my time of versifying,
my time of love, of joyful dreams,
my time of unforced inspiration.
My ecstasy's brief day's no more –
she whom I hymned in veneration
is lost to me for evermore...

translated by Roger Clarke

A Sick Girl

With fragile loveliness she's glowing.
"How long, though? There's no hope," I sigh.
Her youth is like a bloom that's showing,
but as it opens starts to die…
and die it will! She hasn't long now
in her young life to take delight;
nor has she with her presence long now
to bring her dear ones joy and light;
nor will she in our friendly banter
still play her blithe and witty part,
or with her frank and gentle nature
console a sufferer, heart to heart.
I try to hide my apprehensions
(charged though my thoughts are with despair);
I heed her cheerful observations,
savour each precious glimpse of her;
I watch intently every movement,
catch every sound her lips impart,
while dreading in my heart one moment –
that moment when we have to part.

translated by Roger Clarke

A Nereïd

At dawn, amid the waves that kiss Crimea's shore,
a sea nymph rose to sight up from the ocean floor.
Crouching among the trees I held my breath and gazed:
above the limpid sea the demigoddess raised
her young and shapely breasts that gleamed swan-white and bare
and wrung the glistening sea foam from her streaming hair.

translated by Roger Clarke

Crimean Venus

Keen winds are scattering the clouds afar.
O planet that brings sorrow, evening star,
your gleam has touched the autumnal plains with silver,
and the dark rocky banks and sluggish river.
I love you as you shine up there on high:
you've wakened memories I'd long put by.
Familiar star, I watched you rise above
that peaceful land, the whole of which I love,
where slender poplars in the valleys grow
and tender myrtle and dark cypress doze,
and softly plashing southern waves are breaking.
There, deep in thought, a stroll I once was taking
up in the mountains, way above the sea,
when dusk fell on the hamlets of Crimea –
and through the gloom a young star-gazer came
and to her girlfriends called you by her name.

translated by Roger Clarke

Epilogue to *The Fountain of Bakhchisaray*

Eventually I said goodbye
to Petersburg and partying.
I journeyed south and visited
Bakhchisaráy's forgotten palace.
Through noiseless corridors I wandered
to halls where (erstwhile scourge of nations)
the savage Tatar lords had feasted,
after the horrors of their raids,
in indolence and luxury.
Still now a whiff of opulence
lingers in empty rooms and gardens;
fountains still play; red roses bloom;
grape bunches hang from twisting vines;
and gold still glistens on the walls.
I saw the broken lattices
that hid the rooms where, in life's springtime,
the harem wives had inwardly
sighed as they flicked their amber beads.
I saw the graveyard of the khans,
the warlords' final habitation.
Those pillars set above the tombs,
each crowned with turbans carved in stone,
so eloquently, I was thinking,
expressed Fate's final dispensation.
The khans, the harem wives, had gone;
everything there was silent, mournful,
utterly changed... But that was not
what captured my emotions then:
the mesmerizing scent of roses,
the plash of fountains, overwhelmed me;
an unease I could not explain
engulfed my mind; and, as I moved

54

around the palace, there before me
the shadow of a girl kept darting!...

....

Whose shadow was it, friends, I saw?
Tell me, whose gentle apparition
was haunting me with such persistence,
such doggedness, as I walked on?
Could it be chaste Maria's spirit
that I kept glimpsing? Or that fiercely
jealous Zaréma – was it she
that flitted through the vacant harem?

This brings to mind a glance as loving,
a girl as lovely (though still earthbound);
all my affections fly to her –
oh, how I miss her in my exile!
No, madman, that's enough! Desist –
don't reawaken futile yearnings;
for you've already paid your dues to
frustrated love's defiant dreams.
Control yourself. For long enough now
you've kissed your fetters, weary prisoner;
for long enough you've trumpeted
your folly in too-candid verses.

Now I'll serve art and peace anew
and turn my back on fame and love:
yes, soon again I mean to visit
those sunlit valleys of Crimea.
Brimming with private memories,
I'll climb the coastal mountain slopes –
and once again the southern waves
will gladden my impatient eyes.
Enchanted land, a joy to see!

55

All is so vibrant there: hills, woods,
amber and amethyst of grapes,
delightful and secluded dales,
refreshing streams and poplar groves...
All beckons the discerning traveller,
when in the stillness of a morning
he trots his knowing steed along
the rugged path that skirts the shore
and there he sees ahead – not far –
the sea-green swell that breaks and sparkles
below the cliffs of Ayu-Dağ...

translated by Roger Clarke

Tatar Song

from The Fountain of Bakhchisaray

God gives to man in various ways
relief from lifelong woes and tears;
a pilgrim may on Mecca gaze
to soothe the pains of later years.

A fighting man will gain renown
by dying on the Danube's shore;
to greet him flies a houri down,
she smiles: "In heaven we've love in store!"

But luckiest in all Islam –
the man at peace and leisure who,
Zaréma, in the harem's calm
can touch the rose, can fondle you.

translated by Roger Clarke

For the Fountain in the Palace of Bakhchisaráy

Fountain of love and life, flow on!
I've brought two roses for you here.
I love the way you babble on,
spurting your poetry of tears.

Your powdery spray, so silver-pale,
cools me with dewy condensation;
flow, flow, you source of consolation,
murmur to me your mournful tale.

O fount of love, o fount of pity!
I've scanned your stones for news unheard:
some praise I've read of far-off cities,
but of María, not a word...

Pale star that lit the harem chamber,
your presence still we seem to feel –
or are María and Zaréma
mere figments, lovely but unreal?

And was it my imagination
which in the dark, alone and blind,
sketched from a brief hallucination
portraits ideal, but ill-defined?

translated by Roger Clarke

The Rose and the Nightingale

My flawless rose-girl, I'm in bondage;
I'm not ashamed, though, of your bonds:
I'm like a nightingale in foliage,
that feathered tsar of forest song,
who, near the proud and fair rose flower,
stays on in pleasurable duress,
singing to her of tenderness
in love's voluptuous twilight hour.

translated by Roger Clarke

For a Flirt

You surely couldn't have believed me,
as simple-hearted Agnès would have.
Which novel, madam, have you found,
that has a playboy die of love?
Just listen: you are thirty now,
yes, thirty (perhaps a little older);
I'm twenty-one; I've seen the world
and long cavorted in it freely.
I reckon vows and tears a joke now,
and flirting only wearies me –
while you, for your part, must be sick too
of all your infidelities.
Now we're more staid and cooler-blooded,
we shouldn't learn to flirt anew.
We both know well: eternal love
will only last three weeks at most.
It's true that we were friends at first;
but boredom, chance, a jealous husband...
I made as though I were obsessed;
you made as though you were reluctant;
we swore we'd never... Then, alas! —
then we forgot the oaths we'd sworn.
You fell in love with your Cléonte,
and I with my sweet young Natasha.
We went our ways: and till this time
it's all been fine and as it should be.
We could have lived at peace again
as friends, without protracted rows.
But no! This morning suddenly
you feigned an ardour worthy of
a neo-Gothic melodrama –
exhorting us to imitate

the love of valiant knights long-dead,
their courtly passions, griefs and hatreds.
Oh spare me, please! No, no and no!
Poet I may be, child I'm not.
Since we're now both in our decline,
let's leave the fire of young emotions,
you to your adolescent daughter,
I to my younger brother Lev.
They can play games now with their lives
and practise ways of shedding tears.
For them to love is still all right;
for us it's time to vent our spite.

translated by Roger Clarke

Zemfíra's Song

from Gypsies

Husband old and severe,
burn me, slash me, your wife:
I am tough, I've no fear
of the fire or the knife.

You I hate and despise;
it's another I prize;
yes, it's he that I love,
I am dying of love.

Burn me, slash me, your wife:
I shan't say who it is;
husband old and severe,
you won't learn who he is.

He is fresher than spring,
burns like midsummer heat.
He's so young and so brave!
And he loves me a treat!

I have fondled him so
in the still of the night!
And we've laughed at you so,
at your hair thin and white!

translated by Roger Clarke

Shadows of the Past

I've put aside, dear friend, all memory of past years,
of the tempestuous young life that then I led.
Don't question me about those things that are no more,
things given me by Fate to suffer and enjoy,
    things that I loved, and things that played me false.
I cannot now, maybe, experience joy in full;
but you, dear innocent – you're born for happiness:
trust it without reserve; seize every fleeting moment;
your life's been given you for friendship and for love
        and for the ecstasy of kissing.
Your life is pure; to you remorse is alien;
your conscience is a child's, as clear and bright as day:
why should you want to hear a tale of mindless passion,
        a tale of no concern to you?
It can't do other than disturb your peace of mind.
You'll soon be shedding tears and shuddering deep within;
you'll lose your trustfulness and equanimity –
and then, perhaps, my love will cause you to take fright –
take fright, perhaps, for life... Oh no, my dearest girl,
I cannot bear to lose the joys we've lately shared.
Please don't demand of me disclosures that may harm us:
today I have our love, I've joy that's unimpaired.

translated by Roger Clarke

The Tenth Commandment

To crave another's, God above,
you most explicitly forbade me.
You know my limits, though – you made me! –
how can I curb the urge to love?
I'll never wish my neighbour harm,
I do not want his land or chattel,
have no designs upon his cattle;
I view all these with perfect calm.
His house, his ox, his handyman,
I contemplate them undismayed;
but should he have a handy maid
with shapely... Lord, I doubt I can!
And should he have a lovely wife,
fair as an angel (though not flighty),
forgive my weakness, God Almighty,
if I should grudge him his good life.
The heart is free: what is it worth
to undertake what can't be done,
unlove what's loved by everyone,
not covet paradise on earth?
I look, I yearn, but dare not offer
defiance to the stern command;
I quash the heart's remonstrance and
keep silent... and in secret suffer.

translated by Walter Arndt and Roger Clarke

For a Greek Girl

My Greek love, you were born to kindle
the creativity of poets,
and in your winning way to fan
its flames with your vivacious greeting,
your quaint near-eastern mode of speech,
the silvery twinkle of your eye,
and that enticing little foot…
Yes, you were born for idle pleasures,
for sharing the ecstasies of love.
Tell me: when Byron in *The Giaour*
with that sublime inventiveness
portrayed in Leila his ideal,
was it not you that he described
so fondly and so poignantly?
Maybe once, far away beneath
the skies of venerable Greece,
that poet, tortured but inspired,
met you or saw you without knowing,
and hid your unforgettable
image deep down within his soul?
Maybe that sorcerer seduced you
with the enchantment of his verses,
exciting an involuntary
tremor of pride that thrilled your heart,
and you, head resting on his shoulder…
No, no, dear friend, I've no desire
to inflame my thoughts with jealousy.
For long I knew no happiness;
to feel it is a new experience –
though deep forebodings make me fear
that I can't trust what I hold dear.

translated by Roger Clarke

Something or Nothing?

If I were like a child and thrived on joy and hope,
if I could still believe that in due time my soul,
escaping from decay, could carry eternal thoughts,
and memory and love, off into boundless space,
I vow I'd long ago have left this world of ours:
I'd have destroyed this life – foul idol that I worshipped! –
and flown off to a land of freedom and delight,
a land where there's no death, a land without repression,
where thought floats unconstrained beneath unclouded skies.

It's useless, though, to indulge in futile fantasies;
my mind must hold its ground and spurn those idle hopes...
Awaiting me beyond the grave is nothingness...
Nothing at all! No thought, no memory of first love!
In terror and despair, I ponder life anew:
I want now to live long, so that, till I depart,
her image long may glow within my grieving heart.

translated by Roger Clarke

Night

My voice cries out to you with yearning and affection,
troubling the silent hours of night in my dejection.
Beside my lonely bed a candle's glimmering;
and verses through my head are tumbling, murmuring –
fast flowing streams of love, in full spate – overflowing
with you. There in the gloom I see your dear eyes glowing;
they smile at me; and then I hear you softly moan:
"My gentle friend, I love... I'm yours... yes, yours alone..."

translated by Roger Clarke

Jealous Love

Will you forgive my jealous fantasies,
my mindless agitation caused by love?
You're true to me; so why are you so fond
of always scaring my imagination?
You're ever ringed by an admiring throng –
why do you want them all to think you charming?
Why give each one vain hopes with dazzling glances,
from eyes that are now tender, now reproachful?
Now that you've won me, clouded my good sense,
assured yourself that I (alas!) adore you,
don't you observe me in the excited crowd
standing alone, withdrawn and taciturn,
tortured by private hurt and indignation?
For me, no word, no glance... oh cruel friend!
If I should rush away, your eyes don't follow
behind me, apprehensive and appealing.
Or if another gorgeous woman starts
addressing me ambiguous remarks –
you're still relaxed, your cheerful admonition
mortifies me, suggesting you don't love me.
Tell me: when my eternal rival finds me
enjoying a quiet tête-à-tête with you,
why does he greet you with that knowing look?...
What's he to you? What right does *he* have, tell me,
to play the part of pale and jealous lover?...
And late at night, that hour of indiscretion,
why do you need, unchaperoned, alone
and half-undressed, to admit him to your rooms?
But you do love me. When we are alone,
we two, you're so affectionate, your kisses
so full of fire, your words of love

68

so utterly sincere and from the heart!
You make fun of the torment that I feel.
But you do love me – that's to me quite plain.
Dear friend, don't go on torturing me, I beg you:
you don't know with what vehemence I love you,
nor do you know how violent is my pain.

translated by Roger Clarke

Gullible Love

How gullible this heart of ours!
.... worn out once more,
I started lately to implore you
to help in hoodwinking my love –
employ, if need be, sham affection
to animate those gorgeous eyes,
and toy with my subservient soul,
infuse it with your fiery poison.
And you've agreed: you've let your languid
eyes become moist with fond concern.
Your grave and thoughtful countenance,
the open way you talk of love,
the things you tenderly consent to,
the things to which you won't consent –
they're all indelibly incised
upon my deepest consciousness.

translated by Roger Clarke

It's Finished

It's finished; now between us there's no tie.
For one last time I've grovelled at your knees
and, remonstrating, voiced my futile pleas.
It's finished – I can hear your curt reply.
To self-deception I'll now say farewell,
not vex you more with undesired attention;
the past, maybe, will fade from recollection –
love's not for me, I realize now too well.
You're young: you've an attractive disposition;
there's plenty more to fall in love with you.

translated by Roger Clarke

Comparisons

Tumánsky's simile was justified,
    matching you with a rainbow's arc;
you're just as pleasing to the eye,
    and just as volatile at heart.

You're like a rose, as well, that dazzles us in spring;
    you're there before our eyes, unique,
in sumptuous beauty blossoming –
    you also (God forgive you!) prick.

The aptest simile of all, though, I can find
    is spring water; it couldn't please me more;
yes, you're as pure as that in heart as well as mind,
    and colder too than that, for sure.

No other similes are right for such a creature;
the poet's not to blame that nothing matches well.
Such, sadly, are your charms of soul, your charms of feature,
    that you've no parallel.

translated by Roger Clarke

A Storm

That girl upon the rocky shore –
you saw? – in white against the ocean,
amidst the storm-blown breakers' roar,
with land and sea in wild commotion –
time and again a reddish light
illumined her as lightning flashed,
and as the tempest reached its height
her flimsy veil was twirled and lashed.
Awesome, the breakers' crash and roar,
sky, lightning-gashed and overcast;
more awesome's she, though, on the shore
than sea and sky and tempest blast.

translated by Roger Clarke

I V

1824–26

Exile at Mikháylovskoye

Proserpine

Waves on Phlegethon are tossing,
shuddering are Hades' halls.
Pallid Pluto's team of horses
speed the God of Death away
for a tryst with friendly nymphs.

Making her own way behind him
by those empty waters, rode
goddess Proserpine, his consort,
listless, jealous and alone.
In the goddess' path a youngster
shyly dropped down on his knees.
Even goddesses are tempted:
mortal youth took this one's fancy,
so the underworld's proud queen
gave the lad a look of welcome,
took him in her arms, then off they
both sped in her coach to Hades.
Wrapped in cloud they raced along,
through the Blessed Fields, past Lethe's
somnolent and sluggish stream,
lighting in Elysium,
place where heroes live, forgetful,
lives of everlasting bliss.
Proserpine, ecstatic now,
shed her queenly robes and crown,
and, surrendering to desire,
yielded her once hidden beauties
to the youngster's kisses, whilst
swooning in intense delight,
falling silent, faintly moaning...
but love's hours were running short...

Waves on Phlegethon are tossing,
shuddering are Hades' halls.
Pallid Pluto's team of horses
speed the God of Death back home.
Time for Proserpine's departure:
from Elysium she led him,
happy lad, back up to earth
by a footpath little known.
Then the lad, still happy, opened
gingerly the ivory door –
door (alas) that lets swarm through
all those dreams that are not true.

translated by Roger Clarke

The Rain-Quenched Day

The rain-quenched day has died; across the rain-drenched sky
the mists of night unroll their coverings of lead;
just like a ghost, beyond where pines' deep shadows spread
    a misty moon comes rising high...
All, all around me fills my aching soul with tears.
But there, far off, that moon in radiance appears;
there aromatic breaths of evening air blow warm;
there interweaving waves a lavish fabric form;
    there skies of clearest azure soar...
The hour has come! Now down the shadowed cliff she goes
to where the lazy sea laps plashing on the shore;
    there now the one that I adore
sits by our rocks alone, enveloped in her woes...
Alone... There's none to weep before her, nor lament;
none to embrace her knees, his heart with rapture spent;
alone... no other mouth does she allow to kiss
her shoulders, her moist lips, her breasts of snowy white.
....
There's no one can deserve her love, which heaven has sent.
You are alone, I'm sure... in tears... So I'm content.
....
But if.......................

translated by Walter Morison and Roger Clarke

The Desire for Fame

When tenderest love had laid me captive at your feet –
remember, dear? – my wordless rapture was complete.
"Yes, you are mine!" I thought – your eyes were warm and kind!
How could a futile dream of glory cross my mind?
The vain and giddy world had chased me far away:
the poet's calling seemed absurd and childish play.
Wearied by endless storms, why should I ever miss
the tedious buzz of praise, or blame's resentful hiss?
Did rumour's graceless verdicts cloud my spirit when
you laid your gentle hand upon my head again,
your eyes so full of longing? Gently bending near
you whispered, "Do you love me? Are you happy, dear?
Promise you won't forget me... tell me you will never
leave me for someone else... our joy must last for ever..."
My happy heart stood still; bereft of speech, I caught
my breath. In pure delight, I never even thought
that other days could come... the fearful time to part.
But then – what can I say? The pain, the broken heart,
betrayal, slander, torment, tears and bitter shame
engulfed me utterly; and I must bear the blame.
I'm like some traveller, when lightning strikes beside him;
the way ahead is dark, with not a friend to guide him...
Now a new longing comes to set my soul on fire:
the thought of public fame awakens strong desire...
The praise of many mouths will often bring us near;
for when the world applauds, you too are bound to hear.
Then, when my famous name is ringing all around,
you will recall a voice, an urgent, earnest sound:
in darkness in the garden, sad and broken-hearted.
I made my final plea – remember? – as we parted.

translated by John Coutts

Save Me, My Talisman…

Save me, my talisman, I pray,
save me on day of persecution,
day of remorse and retribution:
you were her gift on such a day.

When roaring waves and ocean spray
surge up to break and pound around me,
when flickering thunderclouds surround me,
save me, my talisman, I pray.

When travelling, lonely, far away;
when wearied by folk's peacetime prattle;
when menaced in the heat of battle –
save me, my talisman, I pray.

To bless, delight, then turn away –
bewitching star, what tricks it played me!…
It shone, then vanished and betrayed me…
Save me, my talisman, I pray.

Those inner wounds I bear – may they
not stay inflamed by recollection.
So, Hope, farewell; sleep on, Affection;
save me, my talisman, I pray.

translated by Roger Clarke

The Burned Letter

Letter of love, farewell. Farewell! Yes, she's insisted…
How long now I've held back, how long my hand's resisted
consigning all my joys for ever to the pyre!…
Enough, though. Time is up. O letter, now catch fire.
I'm ready: my numbed mind with nothing now engages,
so let the hungry flames eat up your precious pages…
Alight now! Blazing up! The twisting smoke I see
disperses; with it, too, my unheard litany.
The seal of wax has lost the trusty signet's mark,
it's melting, sizzling – God! the paper's turned quite dark.
It's done! The curled up leaves in blackened fragments rest,
faint now that cherished script which loving words expressed.
Despair constricts my heart. O ash, beloved, forlorn,
though scant relief you give to one who can but mourn,
remain for ever here, against my grieving breast…

translated by Roger Clarke

The Melancholy Moon

The melancholy moon, up there on high,
is meeting with the cheerful dawn, rose-red –
the dawn that's glowing as a youthful bride,
radiant and warm; the moon, though, like one dead,
is cold and pale, as she slips down the sky –
just as I was, Elvína, when we met.

translated by Roger Clarke

Spanish Love Song

The night is clear,
her stars appear.
Roll on, swirl on,
Guadalquivir!

See the golden moon, friend! Waken!
Hear guitar's hushed harmony!
Spanish girl, her room forsaken,
steps out on her balcony.

The night is clear,
her stars appear.
Roll on, swirl on,
Guadalquivir!

Angel! Time to doff mantillas!
Flaunt yourself as brightest day,
and between those iron pillars
cause a pretty foot to stray.

The night is clear,
her stars appear.
Roll on, swirl on,
Guadalquivir!

translated by Roger Clarke

Liza

"Liza's scared to fall in love."
Pah! Don't trust that artful manner.
You beware! This bashful dove,
maybe, is a new Diana,
keeping her desires concealed –
and those sidelong looks so sheepish
are meant coyly to establish
which of you might help her yield.

translated by Roger Clarke

Anna's Name Day

To celebrate with name-day verse
Natálya, Sófya, Kate (or worse!)
is now passé , it seems to us;
but, as a mark of true allegiance
and of unquestioning obedience,
I'm ready to oblige you thus.
But I'll be damned for ever after,
if I know, when they christened you,
why they made "grace" your name thereafter.
No, no, in my considered view,
your pretty foot (and I'm not teasing!),
your way of speech, your downcast face –
they're all exceptionally pleasing;
they lead to ruin, though, not grace.

translated by Roger Clarke

A Confession

I love you – even though insane,
though plagued by pointless shame and pain;
and, wretched in this foolishness,
I kneel before you and confess.
It does not suit my face or age...
It's high time I'd more self-control;
but by my symptoms I can gauge
the lovesickness that blights my soul.
I'm bored, I yawn, when you're away;
I pine, I suffer, when you're here:
and helplessly I yearn to say
how much I love you, angel dear.
When from the drawing room I hear
your dainty step, your rustling dress,
your voice, so innocent and clear,
at once I lose my wits, no less!
You turn away, and how I grieve!
You smile at me, I'm glad again.
It makes up for a day of pain
if your pale fingers brush my sleeve.
When at your needlework you're bent,
so innocently diligent,
with drooping curl and eye so mild,
I'm moved; then, shy and reticent,
I worship you, as would a child!...
Must I admit how sad I feel,
what jealous torment I conceal,
when for an outing off you go,
defying distance, rain or snow?
What of your tears when you're forsaken,
your cosy chit-chats side by side,
those rides to Opóchka that you've taken,

the piano played at eventide?
Alína, angel, pity me!
For love I dare not make a plea;
maybe, for all the wrong I've done
I'm not worth love from anyone.
But just pretend: your lovely eyes
speak words so easily believed;
oh, readily I'll trust their lies,
so glad I am to be deceived!

translated by Roger Clarke

To Praskóvya Ósipova

Maybe I've not long now to stay
here, where I've spent my tranquil exile,
gossiped of times now far away
and, in my poet's quiet way,
indulged in rustic pleasures meanwhile.

But if I reach some foreign state,
I'll still each day in thought be roaming
round your Trigórskoye estate
to see fields, streams and hills, and wait
beneath your lime trees in the gloaming.

Just so, as daylight fades to gloom,
a mournful phantom might come winging
his lonely way from out the tomb
to visit his remembered home
and on his loved ones gaze with longing.

translated by Roger Clarke

To Rodzyánko

To talk more of romanticism
(death of Parnassus' deities!)
and share your home-grown muses' secrets –
that's what you promised me you'd do.
You only write to me of *her*, though…
No, my dear friend, no doubt at all:
Ukrainian rhymester, you're in love!

You're right: there's nothing more important
on this earth than a lovely woman.
Her smiling lips, her glancing eyes –
they far outvalue gold and honour
and ever-controversial praise…
Well then, let's talk again of her.

For sure, friend, I applaud her wish
to take a break and bear some children –
who'll be, I'm sure, their mother's image.
And it's a lucky man who'll share
the joy of such a task with her;
he won't get bored, I'm sure of that!
Let's hope the god of marriage, meanwhile,
will slumber on a good long time!

I disagree with you on this, though:
I'm not in favour of divorce.
Take, first, the vows pronounced in church,
the civil law, the law of nature…
Then secondly (may I point out?)
an upright, honourable husband's
essential for a prudent wife:
for such a man will barely notice,

or even see, a "friend" at home.
Believe me, you fond pair of lovers,
the one liaison aids the other:
marriage's dazzling sun above
helps hide the furtive star of love.

translated by Roger Clarke

To Anna Kern

I well recall a wondrous meeting,
the moment we came face to face –
you, like a vision all too fleeting,
pure spirit of exquisite grace.

Later, in torpor and depression,
in uproar, fuss, fatuity,
I'd catch that voice's soft expression,
dream of those features dear to me.

Time passed. The storms of fierce repression
dispersed those dreams of yesteryear,
drove from my mind your soft expression,
your heavenly features I'd held dear.

In exile's dismal isolation
my days dragged by in misery –
no goddesses, no inspiration,
no tears, no life, no love for me!

Now night has passed, despair's retreating:
once more we're meeting face to face –
you, like a vision still too fleeting,
pure spirit of exquisite grace!

My heart now throbs in exaltation,
exhilarated to attain
its goddess and its inspiration,
its tears, its life, its love again.

translated by Roger Clarke

Sappho

Well-favoured lad, you've won me over by your worth –
your verve, nobility, good nature, all alike –
and those good looks of yours, so fresh, so womanlike.

translated by Roger Clarke

On the Death of Amalia Riznić

Back in her native land, beneath its azure skies,
    she lay worn out, exhausted, dying...
And now she's dead: up there above me, I surmise,
    her young ghost's come already flying.

But there's a line between us crossable by none.
    Sorrow? In vain I've tried to stir it:
from lips that did not care word reached me that she'd gone –
    myself uncaring when I heard it.

So much for her whom once I loved, my heart on fire,
    with such intensity, such sadness,
with such a delicate yet wearying desire,
    and with such torment and such madness!

Where's torment, where's love now? Within me, alas, I find,
    for that poor spirit too approving,
for the sweet memories of days left far behind –
    I find no grieving, nor reproving.

translated by Roger Clarke

V

1826–30

Return to Metropolitan Life

Cleopatra

The hall was glistening. Choirs sang out
accompanied by flutes and lyres.
The Queen's bright voice and sparkling eyes
lent animation to the banquet
and won the hearts of all the guests.
Then all at once, her golden goblet
half-raised, she paused in contemplation,
bowing the head that all admired...

It seemed a trance fell on the feast;
the guests, the singers all fell quiet.
Then once again she raised her brow,
and with unfaltering gaze she spoke:
"You men, will my love give you pleasure?
Then pleasure is now yours to buy...
So listen: I am ready now
to place us all on equal terms.
Who'll come to passion's trading floor?
I offer you my love for sale.
Which of you, tell me then, will buy
one night with me? The price? Your life.

"I vow – oh Mother of Delights,
I'll serve you in a way unheard of:
a common prostitute, I'll mount
my bed and there I'll test their passion.
Hearken to me, then, mighty Venus,
and you too, Lords of the Underworld,
you deities of dreaded Hades,
I vow – until the break of day
voluptuously I'll satisfy
the lusts of those who've purchased me
and slake their appetite for pleasure

with love play known to me alone.
But once divine Aurora's beam
has lit the world with morning purple,
I vow – each lucky suitor's head
shall fall beneath the deadly blade."

She spoke. The guests sat horror-struck,
and hearts began to race with passion...
The company's excited murmur
she heard with air of cold defiance
and scanned with a contemptuous glance
the circle of her devotees...
Then suddenly one man strode forth
from out the throng, then two men more.
Their step was firm; their eyes were fearless;
the Queen rose from her throne to greet them.
The deal was done: three nights were purchased –
such was the fatal bed's appeal.

The banqueters looked on transfixed:
under the blessing of the priests
the lots were drawn now one by one
from out the urn of destiny.
Flavius was first, a doughty warrior,
grown grey in bearing arms for Rome;
he'd been unable to endure
a woman's arrogant disdain,
and so he'd answered to the summons
of pleasure, as in war he'd answered
the summons of a battle cry.
Next Crito, young philosopher,
reared in the groves of Epicurus,
a worshipper and celebrant
of Venus, Cupid and the Graces...
Last, winsome both to heart and eyes,

like a spring flower scarcely opened,
came one who's left posterity
no name. A first soft down still shaded
the youngster's cheeks and chin but lightly;
his eyes, though, gleamed with ecstasy.
The force, still newly felt, of passion
was seething in his youthful heart.
On him Queen Cleopatra rested
a gaze of special tenderness.

And now the light of day is gone,
the golden-hornèd moon is rising;
a soft and restful shade enfolds
the halls of Alexandria.
Fountains are playing, lanterns burning,
a haze of incense drifts aloft,
and breaths of cooler air will soon
refresh the mighty lords of Egypt.
Within a dimly sumptuous chamber,
amidst entrancing masterworks,
canopied round in purple folds,
there stands the glistening couch of gold.

translated by Roger Clarke

The Man I Was Before…

Tel j'étais autrefois et tel je suis encor.

The man I was before, that man I still remain:
light-hearted, quick to love. You know, my friends, it's vain
to think I can observe good looks without elation,
without shy tenderness and secret agitation;
yes, vain to think that love's now toyed with me enough.
In Aphrodite's nets, so delicate yet tough,
like a young hawk have I not writhed, entrapped, constricted?
Unchastened, though, by slights one hundred times inflicted,
I to new idols bring old prayers too well rehearsed…

translated by Roger Clarke

For Nanny

My friend through these last cruel years,
my dear old frail and ageing dove,
alone amidst deep woods of firs
you wait and wait for me in love.
Ever beside your window sitting
as though on watch, you often sigh,
and slower, slower goes the knitting
in those gnarled hands so creased and dry.
You gaze through long-deserted gates
along the dark road far away;
and grief, foreboding, fears, regrets
weigh on your heart throughout the day.
What you imagine...

translated by Roger Clarke

A Riverbank by Night

How glad I am when I can leave behind
the deafening din of capital and court
and slip away into deserted oak woods,
to river banks where these still waters glide.

Now, from the very bottom of the river,
will she soon rise up like a golden carp?

What joy it is when she appears at night,
from out the waves, smooth-flowing in the moonlight!
Her body wrapped around in greenish tresses,
she takes her seat upon the rugged shore.
Beneath her slender, foam-white feet the waters
exchange caresses as they splash and swirl.
Her eyes grow dark, then glisten once again,
like stars that sparkle high in heaven above;
no breath comes from her mouth, but oh, how pungent,
even without a breath, the chilling kiss
planted by those moist lips of deepest blue,
how sweet, how overpowering! – in hot summer
cold mead does not so sweetly quench the thirst.
Whenever with her playful fingers she
tousles my curly hair, immediately
a sudden chill, just like a thrill of terror,
runs through my head, my heart begins to pound;
then, overwhelmed with love, it faints away.
And at that moment I could gladly die;
I want to gasp and gulp down all her kisses –
as for her words… what sound can you compare to
that voice – an infant's earliest utterance,
a purling stream, a skylark's song in May,
a lyre strummed by Boyán the mythic minstrel?

translated by Roger Clarke

The Winter Road

Drifting mists and shifting shadows
part to let the moon break through
and on melancholy meadows
shed her melancholy hue.

Down the winter road (how weary!)
glides the troika, swift, alone,
dinging ceaselessly its dreary
little bell, in monotone.

Songs that coachman Sasha's drawling
bring back memories for me,
now wild revelry recalling,
now a heart in agony.

Empty wastes and snows! No lonely
fire or darkened hut for miles,
but, in dull succession, only
banded posts to mark those miles!

Weary, dreary! But tomorrow,
Nina, I'll return, my friend;
by the fire I'll shed my sorrow,
gazing on you without end.

When the chiming clock's long finger
rounds off twelve resoundingly,
warning late guests not to linger,
midnight won't part you and me.

Nina, I'm so travel-weary;
Sasha's mute, he'll nod off soon;
little bell still dings its dreary
monotone; mists hide the moon.

translated by Roger Clarke

A Correction

No, no: she's no Circassian maid;
to Georgia's lowlands, though, through history
a lovelier girl has never strayed
from towering Kazbek's sombre mystery.

No, in her eyes no agate plays;
yet all the Orient's treasure coffers
could never match the pleasing rays
her sun-bright gaze so sweetly offers.

translated by B. Kelley and Roger Clarke

The Unresponsive Rose

An eastern night in spring, a silent garden's gloom –
there sings a nightingale above a rose in bloom.
But, though he sings, it's plain how unconcerned his rose is:
for all his hymns of love she hangs her head and dozes.
Why then do you assail cold beauty with your song?
Oh poet, show more sense! Why battle on so long?
Will *she* show interest in poets? Not a chance, huh! –
she blooms while you look on; but when you call – no answer!

translated by Roger Clarke

For Yekaterína N. Ushakóva

When people of an earlier day
beheld a ghost or apparition,
they'd drive the Evil One away
with this straightforward admonition:
  "Amen, amen, begone!" But nowadays
such demons, ghouls and ghosts appear to us more rarely
(God only knows where they've all hid themselves away!)
    But you, my good or evil fairy,
    when I see you before me here –
your curly golden hair, your eyes, your lips, your profile –
    and when I hear your voice so clear,
    the words you speak, so bright, so playful,
    I'm hypnotized, I won't deny:
    bewitched by you, I'm fevered, shaking;
    then to myself, not yet quite waking,
  "Amen, amen, begone!" I feebly cry.

translated by Roger Clarke

The Angel

A shining angel, gentle, pensive,
stood radiant by the gates of bliss;
meanwhile a demon, dark, offensive,
flew hovering over hell's abyss.

Spirit of doubt and of negation,
he eyed the radiant soul above
and sensed within, in consternation,
a first reluctant glow of love.

He spoke: "How can I be forgiven?
I've seen your light – it's proved its worth.
I can't hate all there is in heaven,
I can't spurn all there is on earth."

translated by Roger Clarke

The Talisman

Where the sea swell ever surges
seething round deserted cliffs,
where a tranquil moon emerges
through the balmy twilight mists,
where the Muslim takes his pleasure
on a harem girl's divan,
there a sorceress at leisure
gifted me a talisman.

Leisured too was her injunction:
"Keep it safe, my talisman!
It exerts a mystic function.
Love's now given all it can.
Saving you from pain, affliction,
deluge, storm and hurricane,
from disaster and extinction –
not for that my talisman.

"This won't draw in your direction
treasures from far eastern seas;
this won't bring you in subjection
Allah's Prophet's devotees;
nor from dreary foreign places
northward to your native land
will it to a friend's embraces
speed you – not my talisman!

"When a girl, though, slyly glancing,
spellbinds you unknowingly

or at rest, with night advancing,
kisses you unlovingly,
from misjudgements great or little,
from fresh heartache, dearest man,
from bad faith, from slights – then it'll
keep you safe, my talisman."

translated by Roger Clarke

Trinity

For Princess Urúsova

"The Three-in-One," the Church says " – that's what God is."
I'd doubts: a triple god seemed past belief.
Now, seeing you, I've faith, though. What relief!
I can adore three Graces in one goddess.

translated by Roger Clarke

St Petersburg

City of grandeur, squalid city;
fine façades, a jail within;
louring skies of greenish pallor,
    bile and ice and stone –

there's just one thing to your credit:
this – that sometimes down your streets
treads a dainty foot I worship,
    twirls a golden curl.

translated by Roger Clarke

Songs of Georgia

Don't sing, my fair one, when I'm near,
songs of the Georgia I'm regretting;
they bring to mind a bygone year,
a far-off land I was forgetting.

For me they bring to mind, alas! –
those ballads that you sing, so heartless! –
they bring to mind a poor young lass,
her moonlit face, the steppe, the darkness.

On seeing you, I think no more
of that fond, fateful apparition;
but when I hear those songs of yours
her phantom once more clouds my vision.

Don't sing, my fair one, when I'm near,
songs of the Georgia I'm regretting;
they bring to mind a bygone year,
a far-off land I was forgetting.

translated by Roger Clarke

Dedication of *Poltava*

Poltava is for you... but will this
dark story ever catch your ear?
Will you, with your retiring nature,
fathom my feelings, strong, sincere?
Or will this poet's dedication
elicit from you no reply,
as once before his love, unnoticed
and unacknowledged, passed you by?

Do listen to these sounds, this music,
of which you used to be so fond;
then bear in mind: now Fate's betrayed me,
now you've left for the far beyond,
it's that bleak wasteland where you've settled,
that voice of yours I'll hear no more,
that are, alas, all that is left me
to treasure, worship and adore.

translated by Roger Clarke

A Portrait

A temperament that blazes forth,
a heart that's stirred to stormy passion –
she makes appearance on occasion
among you, ladies of the North,
challenging to the very limit
all that society debars,
as does a law-defying comet
amid the nightly-circling stars.

translated by Roger Clarke

Disfavour

When noisy talk makes you the subject,
at your young age, of unfair blame,
and high society's harsh verdict
brings disrepute upon your name,

among the many void of feeling
it's only I who share your pain
and, to a god who's deaf appealing,
pray for you, even though in vain.

Once it has censured indiscretions,
the world does not withdraw its spite;
it only pardons those transgressions
that are committed out of sight.

Show your contempt in equal measure
for their loud-mouthed acclaim and for
their hypocritical displeasure:
best brace yourself to be ignored;

hold those foul vipers in aversion,
avoid the brash, pretentious crew,
avoid their fatuous diversions –
there's one true friend still left to you.

translated by Roger Clarke

A Flower

I've found a flower, dried, unscented,
forgotten in a book I bought,
and questions, random and fragmented,
now crowd out every other thought:

Where did it grow? when? which spring season?
It flowered for long? was picked by whom –
by friend or stranger? What's the reason
that someone chose to press this bloom –

in memory of a fond encounter?
or of a sad, enforced goodbye?
or of a silent, lonely saunter
through fields or shadowed woodlands? Why?

Are he and she alive and wed now?
And have they settled far afield?
Or are the two of them both dead now,
like this strange flower my book concealed?

translated by Roger Clarke

Message from Georgia

The hills of Georgia are veiled in mists of night;
    close by I hear the Arágva flowing.
I'm sad, yet glad at heart; my very sorrow's bright –
    my sorrow that is overflowing
with you, with you alone... There's nothing here to move
    that sorrow into pain, nothing to overpower
my feelings that are now again aflame with love –
    for not to love's beyond their power.

translated by Roger Clarke

For a Kalmyk Girl

Goodbye, my lovely Kalmyk friend,
you almost made me ditch my plans –
I, rightly, like to fraternize and
might have dashed off across the steppes
after that covered cart of yours.
Your eyes, it's true, are narrow slits,
your nose is flat, your forehead wide;
you don't go gabbling on in French,
nor sheathe your slender calves in silk;
you don't cut bread in pretty shapes
beside a teapot, English-style,
nor rave about de Vigny's books,
nor damn poor Shakespeare with faint praise;
you don't resort to meditation
to hide an absence of ideas;
you don't drone arias by Rossini,
nor prance a *galop* at a ball…
No matter! For a full half-hour
as they were harnessing my horses,
your gaze, your beauty from the wilds,
held my attention, mind and heart.
My friends, it surely makes no difference
whether you let your feelings range
in soirées, theatres, bright and smart,
or in a nomad's covered cart.

translated by Roger Clarke

2nd November

It's winter. What's for us to do here in the country?
I greet the man who brings my morning tea with sundry
questions: "How warm is it? Has last night's blizzard stopped?
Does snow lie on the ground, or not? And can I opt
for riding out, or is it best if I inspected,
till lunch, old magazines some neighbour has rejected?"
The snow is lying! So we rise and mount. Away
we canter through the fields at early light of day,
long hunting-whips in hand; keen foxhounds, yelping, follow;
we scan the pallid snow, we scrutinize each hollow,
we trot to left, to right, until, with noon long past,
two hares flushed out and lost, we jog it home at last.
Some fun was that! Night falls; a snowstorm's howling madly;
dimly my candle burns, my heart is aching sadly,
and boredom slowly, drop by poisoned drop, I sip.
I try to read; my eyes along the letters slip,
my thoughts, though, are elsewhere… At last I stop pretending,
take up a pen and sit, intemperately rending
some ill-matched words from my reluctant, weary Muse.
Sound will not fit with sound… At such a time I lose
complete control of Rhyme, my whimsical maidservant:
the lines are feeble, flat – no feeling, no discernment.
Exhausted, I break off my struggle with the lyre
and seek the sitting room; there I can hear the squire
discussing sugar mills and imminent elections;
my hostess, storm-like, casts black looks in all directions,
her steely knitting needles clicking; or she starts
to tell us each our fortunes by the king of hearts.
Oh, life's a bore for those who live in isolation! –
I yearn for a surprise. Maybe in resignation
I'm sitting playing draughts, and then up the approach
there drives a covered sleigh or roomy sledded coach:

out steps a family, a matron and two girls –
curvaceous sisters both, each one with flaxen curls –
how much they'll animate the place till now so numb!
How full, dear God, our lives will all at once become!
At first there'll only pass alert but sidelong glances;
a word or two ensues; then conversation chances
to raise a friendly laugh; a sing-song later on;
vivacious waltzes next; then whispered words lead on
to exchange of melting looks, and snatched flirtatious speeches,
and long encounters up a stairway's narrow reaches.
In the half-dark one girl, unmuffled neck and busts,
steps out onto the porch, face buffeted by gusts –
but icy northern gales won't harm a Russian rose.
How burningly a kiss will glow amidst the frost!
How fresh a Russian girl will bloom among soft snows!

translated by Walter Arndt and Roger Clarke

A Winter's Morning

Look! Frost and sun! A gorgeous morning!
Why sleep as though day's not yet dawning?
Sweet friend, wake up, unseal your eyes
to greet our northerly Aurora,
get out of bed, appear before her,
yourself a star of northern skies.

Recall last night the tempest driving
the snow and heavy storm clouds flying;
you sat so tensely at my side.
The moon, a yellow smudge, was glowing
behind the clouds, but hardly showing –
Today… just take a look outside:

A clear blue sky above! Extended
like sumptuous carpets deep and splendid,
agleam with sunlight, snow now lies;
nothing's left black but leafless forest;
the firs, dark-green, stand thickly frosted;
our little river glints with ice.

This whole room's lit with amber radiance,
and in the hot stove's cosy ambience
you lie stretched out along its ledge,
delighting in the jolly crackle;
but why not have them fetch the tackle
and harness Chestnut to the sledge?

Through morning snow, dear, let's go gliding,
and, headlong after Chestnut flying,
race to the gate and out beyond,
across the fields where there'll be no one,
through woods now leafless, past the millrun –
haunts of which I've so long been fond.

translated by Roger Clarke

Escape

I'm ready. Come my friends, let's travel east or west –
to anywhere at all, wherever you think best.
I'm with you. I intend that haughty Miss to jilt.
Let's go to see the wall those distant Chinese built,
or bustling Paris streets, or, better still, the shore
where gondoliers by night sing Tasso's songs no more,
where ash-embedded stones of ancient cities lie,
and where tall cypress groves breathe fragrance to the sky.
I'm game for anywhere. Let's start, then… But, friends, say:
will my emotions die once I am far away?
will I forget that lass who scorns and tortures me?
Or shall I, to appease the girl's hostility,
still need to render her the homage of my love?…

translated by Roger Clarke

I Loved You

I loved you, and a trace of that love's passion
unquenched within my soul may yet remain;
but my desire is not in any fashion
to sadden you or bring you further pain.
I loved in silence, hopelessly, but dearly,
now shyly, now with jealousy aflame;
I loved you, yes, so fondly, so sincerely –
God grant to you another's love the same.

translated by R.H. Morrison

My Autograph

You want my autograph – but why?
This name will die, a mournful roar
of breaking surf on far-off shore,
or in dark woods a night owl's cry.

My name signed on your album page
will leave a mark that's dead, the same
as when on tombs there's carved a name
in script of a forgotten age.

This name – you'll cease to think of it
when mired in turmoil and dissension,
and of our former friendship it
will bring you no fond recollection.

When lonely, though, in misery,
pronounce it then to ease your grief,
and say: "Someone remembers me;
there's still one heart in which I live."

translated by Roger Clarke

Madonna

I've never wished to adorn a private residence
by hanging wall to wall innumerable old pictures
and have approving guests repeat remarks and strictures
of pompous connoisseurs in awestruck reverence.
But in my simple home, mid half-done tasks piled high,
one painting I'd have wished my eyes could ever savour,
one canvas, out of which there would, as from the sky,
look down on me the holy Virgin and our Saviour,
her eyes with dignity, and *his* with shrewdness, bright –
yes, gently they'd look down, suffused in glorious light,
with them no angel host, just one tall palm of Zion.
My wish is now fulfilled: God in His bounteousness
has vouchsafed you to me as my Madonna icon,
the purest paragon of purest loveliness.

translated by Roger Clarke

Burden of the Past

Whenever in my close embrace
I try to hold your shapely form
and passionately overspend
on you my fund of loving talk,
you say no word, but from my clasp
you ease your supple body free,
and, dearest friend, you answer me
with just a smile of disbelief.
Too zealously you keep in mind
the sad list of my love affairs;
and when I speak, you turn aside,
reproachful, and refuse to hear...
Oh, how I curse those escapades
of my delinquent youth and those
long hours I spent in gardens waiting
by night for secret rendez-vous!
I curse those whispered declarations,
those verses read to girls in vain,
their all-too-credulous caresses,
and tears – when too late to complain.

translated by Roger Clarke

Rhyme

Echo, unable to sleep, was wandering alone by the river.
   Phoebus, that amorous god, spied her and blazed with desire.
Soon the unfortunate nymph grew great with the fruit of his
                                      pleasure;
   whispering Naiads heard groans of a mother-to-be.
Lovely the baby she bore: and Memory, mother of Muses,
   fostered the spirited child, bringing her up with her own.
Sharp and retentive the girl (how very like Echo her mother!),
   friend of the Muses above. Mortals on earth call her "Rhyme".

translated by John Coutts and Roger Clarke

The Page, *or* At the Age of Fifteen

C'est l'âge de Chérubin.

BEAUMARCHAIS

My sixteenth year will soon arrive;
I long to see the joyous day.
Oh, when it comes I'll truly thrive!
Yet even now no man alive
would cast a mocking glance my way.

I'm not a boy – I twirl the hair
upon my upper lip, you see;
I sport an elder's knowing air
and gravel voice, as you're aware...
So watch your step when you're with me.

The ladies like my modest ways,
and one among them steals my breath...
She wields a haughty, languid gaze;
her cheeks with such deep colour blaze
that I for her would suffer death.

She's so commanding and so bold,
she has the most amazing mind –
and jealous – you should hear her scold!
But though you'd find her proud and cold,
alone with me she's warm and kind.

She swore with regal wrath last night
that if I ever dared again
to cast my eye to left or right,
she'd give me poison at the sight –
for that's how much she loves her men!

She's ready, scorning worldly shame,
to fly with me to desert cell.
You'd like to know the lady's name,
my countess from the south of Spain?
Oh no, I swear, I'll never tell!

translated by James Falen

Farewell

Rashly in my imagination
I fondle you, dear, one last time,
dream one last dream of exaltation
and with an anxious, sad elation
one last time call your love to mind.

Our years change, racing on. Unsparing,
they change the world, they change us too.
So now a deathly shroud you're wearing –
that's how you seem to your despairing
poet, and dead he'll seem to you.

Dear distant friend, my heart is aching –
accept this farewell I now send,
like a new widow, heart still breaking,
or one who mutely hugs his shaking
friend to a prison cell condemned.

translated by Roger Clarke

Invocation

Oh, if it's true that in the night –
that time when living souls are sleeping,
when from above the moon's dim light
across the graveyard stones comes creeping –
oh, if it's true that then appear
dead spirits, silent tombs vacating,
I'll summon Leila's ghost; I'm waiting:
come to me, friend, come near, come near!

Appear, ghost, loved by me of old,
as you were at our valediction,
like winter weather, grey and cold,
disfigured by your last affliction;
come, like a star, far off but clear,
like a faint sound, an emanation,
or like some frightening visitation –
no matter how, just come, come near!

I'm summoning you, not for this –
not to expose the shameful history
of why they killed the friend I miss,
nor to explore the grave's grim mystery,
nor yet because sometimes a fear
torments me… no, it's that I mourn you
and want to say I still adore you,
I am still yours: come near, come near!

translated by Roger Clarke

The Promise

You lived among us, then departed
for your dear homeland far away.
I can't forget how, broken-hearted,
I wept and wept with you that day.
My hands, ice-cold and void of feeling,
strove to detain you forcibly;
with choking cries I kept appealing
"Stay on – prolong my agony!"

You firmly, though, cut short my anguished
kisses and disengaged my hand.
You urged: "This land where you've been banished –
now leave it for a brighter land.
And there I'll greet you," you kept saying,
"where skies are ever blue and clear,
where shady olive boughs are swaying.
We'll kiss then one again, my dear."

But there, alas, where sunlight dances
from clear blue skies across the deep,
and where the olives spread their branches –
there you now sleep a lasting sleep.
Your pain, your loveliness too fleeting,
are gone now to the grave below.
But where's that promised kiss of greeting?…
For that I wait still: that you owe.

translated by Roger Clarke

Serenade to Inesilla

I'm here, Inesilla,
I'm here 'neath your room.
Engulfed lies Sevilla
in slumber and gloom.

Cloak, rapier I'm wearing,
and hat with its plume,
guitar too – and daring
to stand 'neath your room.

You're sleeping? Then waken –
I'll strum my guitar.
The old man's awake? Then
he'll learn who we are!

Just hang from your window
a length of silk rope.
You're dawdling within, though –
with no one, I hope!

I'm here, Inesilla,
I'm here 'neath your room.
Engulfed lies Sevilla
in slumber and gloom.

translated by Roger Clarke

Scottish Girl's Song

from A Feast during the Plague

Time was when our peaceful village
seemed a happy, thriving place.
Every Sabbath thankful people
filled the kirk to laud God's grace;
in the schoolroom voices rang out –
ditties by our wee bairns sung;
and across the sunlit meadows
steel blades flashed as scythes were swung.

Now the kirk has lost its people;
school lies silent, locked for good;
fields with uncut corn have ripened;
no one roams the shadowed wood.
Derelict now stands the village,
like an empty, burnt-out mill.
All is quiet; just the graveyard –
that's not empty, that's not still:

all the time they're bringing bodies;
and with wailing those who live
pray in fear that the Creator
to the dead his peace will give.
All the time they need new spaces,
while the tombs of those who sleep
stand together crowding tightly,
like a flock of frightened sheep.

If my springtime's cut off early
blighted by a Fate too drear,
you, whom I have loved so dearly,
you, whose love's my only cheer,

keep away from your dead Jenny,
I implore you; don't come near;
don't press my cold lips with kisses;
follow far behind my bier.

Then depart this stricken village;
go away, go anywhere
where you may find rest and comfort
and relieve your soul's despair.
When the plague's past, then, dear Edmund,
come, greet my poor dust so fond;
Jenny will stay true to Edmund
even in the world beyond.

translated by Roger Clarke

VI

1831–37

Marriage and Final Years

A Different Kind of Love

No, those wild joys I now renounce without complaint –
the body's fierce desire, delirium, unconstraint,
the groans, the frenzied cries a young bacchante'll make
as, tight within my arms but writhing like a snake,
she scars me with each kiss and sears me with her clasping,
climaxing fast our spasms of shuddering and gasping.

My dear submissive one, how much more I love you!
How painfully intense the joy I feel with you,
when, bending to my long and eager supplication,
you yield yourself to me in gentle resignation;
first, frigid and abashed, you show no satisfaction
with my aroused desire, you offer no reaction;
and then you come to life, a little now, then more –
and share at last my fire that left you cold before!

translated by Roger Clarke

Second Meeting

for the Album of Princess A. D. Abamelék

Once (this brings back a warm sensation!)
I cradled you in admiration –
a gorgeous baby you were then.
You've blossomed now – in veneration
I greet you, now we meet again.
My heart and eyes fix their attention
on you; I quiver deep inside;
and in both you and your perfection,
like an old nursemaid, I take pride.

translated by Roger Clarke

Memory of Moscow

an album verse

Far from old Moscow and its pleasure,
banished by fate, to live I'm doomed;
but in my heart I'll always treasure
the city where your flower has bloomed.
The din of Petersburg distracts me;
to a wretched life I'm here consigned –
the thought of you alone attracts me
and brings dear Moscow back to mind.

translated by Roger Clarke

Name-Day Greeting

an album verse

Blank still are your precious pages,
buried on this desk of mine.
Your poor album's lain long ages
(sorry! – it quite slipped my mind)
empty, uninscribed, unsigned.
Now your nameday's here, my pleasure
is – today! – to wish you, dear,
much to cherish, much to treasure,
much to offer you good cheer –
much acclaim for verses written,
many days at peace to spend –
and a conscience never smitten
by an album still unpenned,
lent by such a lovely friend.

translated by Roger Clarke

A Beautiful Woman

an album verse

In her all's heavenly harmony,
in her no wanton worldliness;
she rests serenely, modestly,
triumphant in her loveliness.
And when she casts her gaze around her,
she finds no rivals there, not one;
she far outshines that set of wan
Petersburg beauties who surround her.

Wherever, friend, you're hurrying,
perhaps to a lovers' assignation,
whatever dream you're nurturing
deep down in your imagination –
if you meet her (a sight sublime!)
you'll falter in incomprehension
and, with a worshipper's intention,
kneel pilgrim-like at Beauty's shrine.

translated by Roger Clarke

Detachment

I must not, cannot, do not dare
insanely yield to passion's pains;
I guard my inner calm with care
and keep my sober heart in chains.
Though done with love, am I not free
to dream a passing dream at times,
when accidentally I see
a pure, angelic girl go by
and disappear?... And can't I then,
admiring her with longing gaze,
pursue her with my eyes and send
a prayer to bless her all her days,
and wish her goodness from above,
and happiness and peace in life –
yes, even joy for him she'll love,
who'll call the charming girl his wife?

translated by James Falen

The Baron's Return

Late at night a lord comes riding…
Watch him, through the castle striding:
(see the servants shake with dread)
first, the bedroom… well-suspected! –
next, the curtains – as expected,
no one there: an empty bed!

Lord of Poland's plains, victorious,
shrewd in love, in battle glorious,
twirls his grey moustache, and then
tests the lock, his eyes half-closing,
and, filled now with dark supposing,
bellows, "Are you dogs or men?

"You – my serf – suggest a reason
why the door stands wide – what treason
chained the guard-dogs?… Stupid brute!
Did we try to fool our betters?
Bring a musket, knife and fetters;
let me teach you how to shoot…"

Lord and lad go scouting, keeping
stealthy lookout, slowly creeping
through the trees at dead of night.
In the grove, despising danger,
stands a young unhappy stranger;
sits a lady dressed in white.

Now he whispers: "All is perished –
all the love I vainly cherished,
all the happiness I sought…
tender touch of gentle fingers
(how the sad remembrance lingers!…)
All I've lost the baron's bought.

"Through the years I wooed you plainly,
through the years I served you vainly:
all my yearning passed you by.
Did the baron's heart lie bleeding?
Silver coins rang loudly, pleading.
You accepted. Tell me why...

"Through the darkness I have ridden,
ever faithful, still unbidden,
all to kiss your tender hand...
May my sorrows touch you never!
Soon I'll say farewell for ever;
soon I'll seek a foreign land."

While he kneels before her, sighing,
hears her long and bitter crying,
lurking spies prepare the gun:
pour the powder – killing's fuel –
load the bullet – round and cruel –
ramrod home! – the job is done.

"Master, please, why did you choose me?...
I'm a wretched shot – excuse me..."
frightened serf now tries to say.
"Eyes are stinging – hands are shaking:
what a noise the wind is making...
half the powder's blown away."

"Quiet, you whining fool! Tomorrow
be prepared to taste some sorrow.
Check the powder: take your aim...
Left a little... see the beauty?
Higher... Kill her. Do your duty.
Leave the other... he's my game."

Then a sudden shot resounded.
Both the lovers stood dumbfounded;
someone shrieked and fell down dead.
Yes, the lad was primed and ready,
held the musket straight and steady,
shot his master through the head.

translated by John Coutts

Beauty's Power

To ache with love, I thought, downhearted,
I've lost my old propensity.
"That which I used to be," I started
to say, "the same I'll never be."
Love's joys and pains – they'd stopped occurring,
and dreams too easy to believe…
But now once more I feel them stirring –
so much can Beauty's power achieve!

translated by Roger Clarke

Charming Lad

after the Arabic

Charming lad, so young and tender,
mine for ever, have no shame;
rebels both, we won't surrender,
life has made us both the same.
I don't mind the constant mocking:
two can bear it twice as well;
we're twin walnuts interlocking,
wrapped inside a single shell.

translated by James Falen

Fragment from Anacreon

from A Tale of Roman Life

Mettled steeds you'll recognize
by the brand scorched on their hides;
Parthian lords you'll recognize
by their turbaned heads held high.
I, though, always recognize
happy lovers by their eyes:
in them glows a languid fire –
proof of gratified desire.

translated by Roger Clarke

Worldweariness

It's time, my dear, it's time! For peace my heart's appealing –
day chases after day; each passing hour is stealing
a scrap of what we are. We're planning, you and I,
together to live on. Reflect, though: soon we'll die.
On earth here there's no bliss. But peace and independence
there are; long in my dreams I've craved such an existence –
yes, long back, weary serf, I thought of taking flight
to a refuge far away of work and pure delight.

translated by Roger Clarke

Editor's Note

Titles

Identifying Pushkin's love poems in a consistent manner presents the editor with problems. Many of the poems were not given titles by Pushkin, or were given quite unhelpful titles such as "To Her" or just "To ***". To help the reader, therefore, I have given those poems without a specific title a title of my own. For each poem, the Russian title that Pushkin used (if he did) and the first line in Russian are provided in the notes.

The translations

Our intention has been to present Pushkin's poems in clear and natural modern English, unobscured by archaic or obsolete "poetic" language. This, we felt, would be truest to Pushkin's own normally direct and informal style, as well as being most accessible to today's English reader. Ninety-four of the translations here are mine (including six previously published elsewhere); five are by Professor James Falen; four are by John Coutts; and one each are by Mary Hobson, David and Lyudmila Matthews, and R.H. Morrison. The remaining seven are others' versions that I have substantially amended, so they are presented here as joint translations. Readers wishing to look up the relevant original Russian texts will be able to find them on the Alma Classics website: www.almaclassics.com/lp/lovepoems.pdf.

You and you

Russian, like French, has two second-person pronouns, *ty* and *vy*; and their usage is similar to the French *tu* and *vous*. *Ty* only addresses one person; in Pushkin's day it was used primarily among family members and close friends or to social inferiors, implying a certain degree of intimacy or informality. The other pronoun, *vy*, is always used when addressing more than one person. Pushkin and his contemporaries would also use *vy* for single individuals when they were not on intimate terms, were signalling respect, or wished to distance themselves. It is almost impossible to bring this distinction out in modern English, where the pronoun "you" is the only one available. In this book the assumption should be that Pushkin always uses the second-person pronoun *ty*; in the minority of cases where Pushkin uses *vy*, this is noted in the commentary.

Transliteration

I have used the simplified British Standard system for the trans-literation of Russian names. For non-Russian names I have used the corresponding modern national orthography. Russian and Polish women are referred to by the female form of their surnames. Because of the importance of stress in the correct pronunciation and scansion of Russian, and of its unpredict-ability, I have regularly marked (except in titles of works) the stressed syllable of Russian names with an acute accent over the relevant vowel; the only exceptions are names of one syllable, and those of two syllables where the stress falls on the first (e.g. Pushkin).

Metre

Pushkin most often used an iambic rhythm (ᴗ –) for his verses; and the commonest metre he used for the poems in this volume was the iambic tetrameter, i.e. four iambs (strong ending), or four iambs followed by an extra weak syllable (weak ending):

$$\cup - \cup - \cup - \cup - (\cup)$$

Sometimes he used five iambs to a line (pentameter) or six iambs (hexameter), always with the option of an extra weak syllable at the end; and occasionally he used lines of three iambs (trimeter) or even two (dimeter). With a hexameter line he would normally place a caesura (word break) after the sixth syllable. Sometimes he mixed lines of different lengths.

In a minority of cases (usually for humorous, invective or folkloric verse) Pushkin used a trochaic rhythm ($- \cup$), again usually in groups of four trochees, with the final weak syllable optional:

$$- \cup - \cup - \cup - (\cup)$$

Only in one instance in this volume ('Rhyme') does Pushkin use a dactylic rhythm ($- \cup \cup$), in imitation of Greco-Roman verse. Uniquely, too, Zemfira's savage song from *Gypsies* is in anapaestic dimeters ($\cup \cup - \cup \cup -$).

Our normal practice has been to replicate Pushkin's metres, though sometimes substituting strong endings for his weak ones. Where we have departed from this practice I have drawn attention to it in the commentary.

Rhyme

Pushkin habitually rhymes all his lines. The rhymes are variously arranged in pairs (AABB CCDD, etc.), alternately (ABAB CDCD, etc.), in ring form (ABBA CDDC, etc.) or in a mixture of these. In these cases A will normally represent a weak line ending, and B a strong ending, or vice versa. When poems are arranged in five-line or six-line stanzas the pattern will be more complex. In narrative poems and other longer pieces Pushkin's rhyme scheme is often irregular and unpredictable. There are only two instances of poetry unrhymed by Pushkin in this volume – 'A Riverbank by Night' and (paradoxically) 'Rhyme'.

Fully rhymed English translations are problematical, however. Because of the uninflected nature of the English language (nouns and verbs mostly lacking regular endings) and the rigidities of English word order, it is much harder to find natural rhymes in English than in Russian, particularly for weak line endings. Despite this, the present translators have striven to produce faithful and fluent versions that in most cases still replicate Pushkin's rhyme schemes. Witty epigrams lose their pointedness without rhyme, and unrhymed translations of song-like poems written in regular stanzaic form will not do justice to the formal beauty of Pushkin's originals. Sometimes we have compromised slightly by rhyming every other line (as frequently in English poetry) where Pushkin has rhymed each line, and in a minority of cases (e.g. where Pushkin's own rhyme scheme is irregular) the translation is presented as unrhymed verse.

Dates

Dates refer to the Julian ("Old Style") calendar, which was in force in Russia during the nineteenth century.

– Roger Clarke

Notes and Commentary

p. 5, *Reason and Love* (*Рассудок и Любовь / Младой Дафнис, гоняясь за Доридой...*): One of Pushkin's earliest extant poems, written when he was fourteen in the tradition of French pastoral poetry. It was first published (without his permission) in 1835. The translator has slightly altered Pushkin's rhyme scheme and has used iambic tetrameters instead of Pushkin's lengthier pentameters.

p. 6, *The Tear* (*Слеза / Вчера за чашей пуншевою...*): Written in 1815, and first published in 1825 in a musical setting.

p. 7, *For the Lovely Girl who Took Snuff* (*Красавице, которая Нюхала Табак / Возможно ль? вместо роз, Амуром насажденных...*): The poem dates from 1814; it was unpublished in Pushkin's lifetime. The addressee is understood to have been Princess Yeléna Mikháylovna Kantakúzena (1794–1854), married sister of A.M. Gorchakóv, one of Pushkin's classmates; Pushkin would have met her visiting her brother in the school. Pushkin's original is fully rhymed on an irregular pattern; the translation is unrhymed, but adopts a similar iambic metre to Pushkin's, with lines, like his, of varying length. The name Kliména (French *Clymène*, Greek *Clymenē*), which Pushkin uses to disguise the real addressee, derives from classical mythology: the original Clymenē goes back to Homer, where she was an attendant to Helen (Russian Yeléna) of Troy.

p. 9, *To a Young Widow* (*К Молодой Вдове / Лида, друг мой неизменный...*): Written early in 1817; unpublished in Pushkin's lifetime. The poem was addressed, under the classical pseudonym Lida, to a Frenchwoman called Marie Smith. Recently widowed but expecting a child, the young and attractive Madame Smith had come to stay with the family of the Lycée's director. The young Pushkin, smitten by her, composed this verse message fantasizing his love and then presented it to her. Not surprisingly, Madame Smith was much put out and showed the poem to the director, who reprimanded Pushkin severely.

p. 11, *To Elvína* (*К Ней / Эльвина, милый друг, приди, подай мне руку...*): Written in 1815 or 1816; first published in 1817. Another love fantasy. Elvína was the attractive young heroine of a ballad written in 1814 by the eminent poet Vasíly Andréyevich Zhukóvsky (who later became Pushkin's friend and mentor). Pushkin used the name several times in his poetry to address fictional women friends, or real ones whose identity he wished to conceal.

p. 12, *The Moon* (*Месяц / Зачем из облака выходишь...*): Written in 1816, unpublished in Pushkin's lifetime.

p. 13, *To Morpheus* (*К Морфею / Морфей, до утра дай отраду...*): Written in 1816 and first published in 1824.

p. 14, *To Friends* (*Друзьям / Богами вам еще даны...*): Written in 1816 and first published in 1826.

p. 15, *The Singer* (*Певец / Слыхали ль вы за рощей глас ночной...*): This delicate pastoral piece was written in 1816 and first published a year later. Thereafter it was several times set to music, notably (in a shortened form) by Tchaikovsky for the Larin sisters' duet at the beginning of his opera *Eugene Onegin*. The second-person pronoun used in this song is the plural (or formal) *vy*.

p. 16, *Cupid and Hymen* (*Амур и Гименей / Сегодня, добрые мужья...*): Written in 1816 and first published in 1826. The translator has replaced Pushkin's iambic tetrameters with a trochaic rhythm. In Greco-Roman mythology Vulcan, the blacksmith god, was married to Venus, goddess of love; according to Pushkin's version, they had two sons, the stolid Hymen, god of marriage, and the mischievous youngster Cupid (or Eros), god of free love, who sprouted wings and carried a bow, habitually shooting his arrows blindfold.

p. 18, *A window* (*Окно / Недавно темною порою...*): Written in 1816; unpublished in Pushkin's lifetime.

p. 19, *Her* (*Она / «Печален ты; признайся, что с тобой»*): Written in 1817; unpublished in Pushkin's lifetime.

p. 20, *Notice on the Infirmary Wall* (*Надпись на Стене Больницы / Вот здесь лежит больной студент;*): Written in June 1817; unpublished during Pushkin's lifetime. When his schoolfriend I.I. Pushchin was lying ill in the infirmary, Pushkin as a joke inscribed this verse on a board at the bedhead.

p. 21, *For Delivery to the Bábolovsky Palace* (*На Баболовский Дворец / Прекрасная! пускай восторгом насладится...*): Written probably in 1816; unpublished in Pushkin's lifetime. This verse is addressed to Sófya Iósifovna Vélyo (1793–1840), a woman of striking beauty who became mistress to the Emperor Alexander I. The couple used to meet at the Bábolovsky Palace in a remote part of the park surrounding the main summer palace at Tsárskoye Seló just outside St Petersburg, in a wing of which Pushkin's school was located. Alexander (the "demigod") was at this time (the mid-1810s) at the height of his power and prestige in Europe following the overthrow of Napoleon.

p. 25, *Friendship and Love* (* * * / *И я слыхал, что божий свет...*): Found in rough draft in Pushkin's papers; probably written late 1818 or early 1819.

p. 26, *Yours and Mine* (* * * / « Tien et mien, — dit Lafontaine...»): Written by Pushkin in French:

> "Tien et mien," dit Lafontaine,
> "du monde a rompu le lien."
> Quant à moi, je n'en crois rien.
> Que serait-ce, ma Climène,
> si tu n'étais plus la *mienne*,
> si je n'étais plus le *tien*?

The verse was never published in Pushkin's lifetime. Pushkin has in mind a fable ('La Discorde', Book VI, no. 20) by the French writer Jean de La Fontaine (1621–95) which names "Yours-and-Mine" as the goddess Discord's father. According to the fable, the gods, angry at the trouble Discord had caused in heaven, banished her to earth, where she continued to spread dissension and havoc, notably between married couples. For Clymène, see note on 'For the Lovely Girl Who Took Snuff' above. A Clymène was also the heroine of a short pastoral comedy on the subject of love by La Fontaine himself.

p. 27, *Ye Gods!* (* * * / *Как сладостно!.. но, боги, как опасно*): A rough draft of 1818, unpublished in Pushkin's lifetime. The addressee is unknown.

p. 28, *To Yelizavéta Ogaryóva* (*К Огаревой, которой Митрополит прислал плодов из своего саду / Митрополит, хвастун бесстыдный...*): Written in August 1817 and unpublished in Pushkin's lifetime. Yelizavéta ("Lisabet") Sergéyevna Ogaryóva (1786–1870) was a St Petersburg beauty and the wife of a senator, whom Pushkin had first met (and admired) at Tsárskoye Seló in the summer of 1816. The word translated *bishop* in fact denotes a "metropolitan", who in the Orthodox Church hierarchy ranks above archbishop. Pushkin is referring to Ambrósy, Metropolitan of Nóvgorod and St Petersburg (1742–1818). By *pro-creation's deity* Pushkin means Priapus, in Greco-Roman mythology god of fertility, including not only fruitfulness but also male sexual potency; his phallic image was often placed in Roman gardens. The joke was that Metropolitan Ambrósy was actually an already frail seventy-five-year-old.

p. 29, *My Homeland* (* * * / *Краев чужих неопытный любитель...*): Written on 30th November 1817 and unpublished in Pushkin's lifetime. The subject of this poem, Princess Yevdókiya (Avdótya) Ivánovna Golítsyna (1780–1850), was the hostess of an eminent literary salon in St Petersburg, attended by the leading Russian writers of the day. She was known both for her beauty and for her Russian patriotism, which led her to espouse liberal political views and to favour the establishment of constitutional government for Russia. The young Pushkin was strongly attracted to her and frequented her salon at this period.

p. 30, *For Princess Golítsyna* (*Княгине Голицыной,посылая ей оду «Вольность»* / *Простой воспитанник природы...*): At the end of 1817 Pushkin had composed one of his most famous political poems, the ode 'Freedom', attacking injustice, serfdom and tyranny. He subsequently presented a copy of this ode to Princess Yevdókiya Golítsyna (see note on 'My Homeland' above), under cover of this elegant and tongue-in-cheek message. He respectfully addresses the Princess with the formal pronoun *vy*, not the more intimate *ty*. The verse was unpublished during Pushkin's lifetime.

p. 31, *Madrigal for M—* (*Мадригал М....ой* / *О вы, которые любовью не горели...*): First published in 1820. The translation replaces Pushkin's iambic hexameters with pentameters. The addressee is unknown.

p. 32, *To A. B—* (*К. А. Б**** / *Что можем наскоро стихами молвить ей?...*): First published in 1826. The translation replaces Pushkin's iambic hexameters in the first and third lines with pentameters. The addressee is unknown.

p. 33, *For Catherine Bakúnina* (*Бакуниной* / *Напрасно воспевать мне ваши именины...*): Yekaterína ("Catherine") Pávlovna Bakúnina (1795–1869) was the elder sister of one of Pushkin's classmates at the Imperial Lycée, and he had been infatuated with her from his school-days. Nevertheless, in this poem he still respectfully addresses her, as an older woman, by the formal pronoun *vy*, not by the more intimate *ty*. St Catherine's day is celebrated in the Russian Orthodox Church on 24th November, and Pushkin would have written this piece, no doubt for inclusion in her album, for that date in 1818 or 1819. The verse was unpublished during Pushkin's lifetime.

p. 34, *To Shcherbínin* (*К Щербинину* / *Житье тому, любезный друг...*): Written on 9th July 1819; unpublished in Pushkin's lifetime. Pushkin's lines are rhymed in an irregular pattern. Mikhaíl Andréyevich Shcherbínin (1793–1841) was an officer friend of Pushkin's. The poem, composed as a letter in verse, gives a picture of the extravagant and uninhibited lifestyle of Pushkin and his circle at this period. *Strasbourg pâté*, an imported delicacy, was a pâté of goose livers larded with truffles.

p. 35, *For Olga Masson* (*О. Массон / Ольга, крестница Киприды...*): Written in 1819; unpublished in Pushkin's lifetime. Olga Masson was one of the St Petersburg "ladies of the night", frequented by Pushkin and his friends.

p. 36, *That's When She'll Come...* (* * * / *Она тогда ко мне придет...*): This verse, plausibly attributed to Pushkin, is known only from later copies.

p. 37, *Recovery* (*Выздоровление / Тебя ль я видел, милый друг?...*): Written in 1818, after Pushkin had been ill, and first published in 1826. Addressed to another "lady of the night", Yelizavéta Schott-Schedel, nicknamed Delfíra by Pushkin elsewhere, who visited the sick Pushkin in hospital, cross-dressed in military uniform. It seems she dropped him afterwards, because Pushkin refers to her bitterly in the opening lines of the Fifth Canto of *Ruslan and Lyudmila*.

p. 38, *Dorída – and Another* (*Дорида / В Дориде нравятся и локоны златые...*): Written in 1819 and first published in 1820. Dorída (Greek *Dōris*) is probably a classical pseudonym for one of Pushkin's girlfriends, perhaps the one addressed in the opening lines of the Sixth Canto of *Ruslan and Lyudmila*, who apparently disowned him at the time of his banishment to the South (see Epilogue to *Ruslan and Lyudmila* in Part II on p. 49).

p. 39, *Trustful Love...* (*Дориде / Я верю: я любим; для сердца нужно верить.*): Written in late 1819 or early 1820; first published 1820. Apparently addressed to the same girl as mentioned in the last poem.

p. 40, *Platonic Love* (*Платонизм / Я знаю, Лидинька, мой друг...*): Written in 1819. Binyon identifies the addressee as the young Polish girl Sofya Potocka (later Sofya Kiselyóva – 1801–75), who was much admired at this time by Pushkin and his friends. Pushkin intended to include the poem in his first collection of published verses in 1825, but withdrew it at a late stage because he "wanted to be a moral chap". It remained unpublished during his lifetime. For *winged boy-god* and *brother Hymen* see note on 'Cupid and Hymen' above.

p. 42, *In Sosnítskaya's Album* (*В Альбом Сосницкой / Вы съединить могли с холодностью сердечной...*): Written probably in 1819; unpublished in Pushkin's lifetime. Yeléna Yákovlevna Sosnítskaya (1800–55) was a popular and attractive young opera singer and actress, already married at this time to a fellow actor. Though she revelled in the admiration of others, contemporaries regarded her as cold at heart. Pushkin here respectfully addresses her by the formal pronoun *vy*, suggesting that they were not yet on intimate terms.

p. 43, *Aimed at Kólosova* (*На Колосову / Все пленяет нас в Эсфири...*): Written in 1819; unpublished in Pushkin's lifetime. Alexandra Mikháylovna Kólosova (1802–80) was another celebrated young actress, who had previously won Pushkin's admiration. In 1819 she appeared in St Petersburg as Esther, the biblical Jewess who became Queen of Persia, in Racine's eponymous tragedy. Pushkin, however, thought Kólosova more suited to comic roles, and preferred another actress in tragic parts. He later regretted his tactless epigram – see next poem.

p. 44, *For Katénin* (*Катенину / Кто мне пришлет ее портрет...*): This short verse letter, completed on 5th April 1821 and published in 1826, seeks to make amends for the offence caused by the previous poem. It is addressed to the poet, critic and dramatist Pavel Alexándrovich Katénin, a friend both of Pushkin's and of the actress Kólosova; Pushkin was hoping that Katénin would effect a reconciliation. *Célimène* was a role played by Kólosova in Molière's comedy *Le Misanthrope*, and *Moïna* was the leading female role in the Russian playwright Vladisláv Alexándrovich Ózerov's tragedy *Fingal*, a part she had played in 1818.

p. 45, *Song of the Twelve Girls* (*Песня Двенадцати Дев, из Руслана и Людмилы / Ложится в поле мрак ночной...*): For *Ruslan and Lyudmila* see *Alexander Pushkin's life: St Petersburg 1817–20* on p. 180. A passage near the beginning of the Fourth Canto parodies a lengthy ballad, *The Twelve Sleeping Maidens*, by Pushkin's friend and mentor the poet Vasíly Andréyevich Zhukóvsky (1783–1852). This ballad tells of a remote castle on the Dnieper inhabited by twelve maidens whose destiny it is to sleep there until a noble warrior arrives and falls in love with one of them; every month one of the twelve girls takes her turn to wait on the battlements and watch for the approach of the hero while her eleven sisters sleep. In Pushkin's version the girls are wide awake, keenly awaiting the arrival of any man who comes their way; Pushkin has the sister on duty on the battlements sing this song, as she spots a young warrior approaching.

p. 49, *Epilogue to* Ruslan and Lyudmila (*Руслан и Людмила – Эпилог / Так, мира житель равнодушный...*): Though Pushkin had completed *Ruslan and Lyudmila* before the government expelled him from St Petersburg, it was published in his absence. When he reached the Caucasus that summer, he composed an autobiographical epilogue to the main work; in it he expresses shock and despair at his sudden change of fortune, including his desertion by Dorída, presumably the same girl that he had celebrated so enthusiastically in the poems 'Dorída – and Another' and 'Trustful Love' months before. The epilogue reached St Petersburg too late to be printed with the first edition of the main work and was published separately later in the year; it was included with *Ruslan and Lyudmila* in subsequent editions.

p.　51, *A Sick Girl* (* * * / *Увы! зачем она блистает...*): Written in 1820, and first published in 1823. Almost certainly addressed to Yekaterína Rayévskaya – for whom see *Alexander Pushkin's Life: Travels in the South 1820* on p. 181.

p.　52, *A Nereïd* (*Нереида* / *Среди зеленых волн, лобзающих Тавриду...*): Written towards the end of 1820 and first published in 1824. Pushkin is almost certainly spying on Yekaterína Rayévskaya – see above. In classical mythology the Nereïds were sea nymphs, daughters of Nereus, a sea god.

p.　53, *Crimean Venus* (* * * / *Редеет облаков летучая гряда...*): Written at Kámenka on the lower Dnieper in the Ukraine in late autumn 1820; first published in 1824. The reference in the final lines is to Yekaterína Rayévskaya (see *Alexander Pushkin's Life: Travels in the South 1820* on p. 181). Yekaterína, who was proud of her looks, sometimes used to call herself "Venus". To avoid embarrassment vis-à-vis Yekaterína, who by 1824 was married to another man, Pushkin asked the publisher to suppress the last three lines, but the publisher, to Pushkin's annoyance, disobeyed.

p.　54, *Epilogue to* The Fountain of Bakhchisaray (*Бахчисарайский Фонтан – Эпилог* / *Покинув север наконец...*): Pushkin's narrative poem *The Fountain of Bakhchisaray* was written between 1821 and 1823 and published in 1824. The story is an oriental romance, in Byronic style, set in the palace of the Tatar khans in Bakhchisaráy, which Pushkin visited with the Rayévskys during his Crimean holiday, some forty years after its conquest by the Russians. The story concerns the love of a Tatar khan for two of his harem wives, both of whom have been kidnapped by Tatar raiders from their homelands: one is a shy, devoutly catholic Polish princess called María, and the other a hot-blooded, voluptuous Georgian girl known as Zaréma. The story ends with the deaths of both girls and with the khan's installation in the palace of a new wall fountain (the still-extant "fountain of tears") in memory of María. As with *Ruslan and Lyudmila*, Pushkin added an autobiographical epilogue. The paragraph beginning *This brings to mind a glance as loving...* refers again to Pushkin's recollections of Yekaterína Rayévskaya, now married and out of reach – see note on preceding poem. *Ayu-Dağ* ("Bear Mountain") is a precipitous headland jutting into the Black Sea just east of Gurzúf.

p.　57, *Tatar Song* (*Татарская Песня, из Бахчисарайского Фонтана* / *Дарует небо человеку...*): For *The Fountain of Bakhchisaray* see previous note. This song Pushkin put into the mouths of the Tatar khan's slave girls at Bakhchisaráy; it celebrates Zaréma, the khan's recent favourite among his harem wives.

p. 58, *For the Fountain in the Palace of Bakhchisaráy* (*Фонтану Бахчисарайского Дворца* / *Фонтан любви, фонтан живой...*): This lyric, written in 1824 and published two years later, again draws on Pushkin's memories of his visit to Bakhchisaráy in 1820. For Bakhchisaráy, María, Zaréma and the "fountain of tears" see previous two notes. *Some praise I've read of far-off cities*: one of the inscriptions above the fountain, in Ottoman Turkish, includes words praising the beauty of Damascus and Baghdad.

p. 59, *The Rose and the Nightingale* (* * * / *О дева-роза, я в оковах...*): First published in 1826, when Pushkin described it as "in the style of a Turkish song" and hinted that it was inspired by his travels in the Crimea in 1820.

p. 60, *For a Flirt* (*Кокетке* / *И вы поверить мне могли...*): Written in 1821; unpublished in Pushkin's lifetime. It is addressed to Agláya (Aglaë) Antónovna Davýdova (1787–1842), the promiscuous wife of Alexánder Lvovich Davýdov – see *Alexander Pushkin's Life: Travels in the South 1820*, p. 182. Pushkin emphasizes his contempt by addressing Aglaë by the formal pronoun *vy*. *Agnès* is a gullible young girl in Molière's *L'École des femmes*. *Cléonte* is an eligible middle-class bachelor in Molière's *Le Bourgeois gentilhomme*, who, to overcome snobbish opposition to his marriage, pretends to be a son of the Turkish Sultan. Pushkin is suggesting that Aglaë's lover (whoever he was) was a *poseur* with pretensions above his rank.

p. 62, *Zemfíra's Song* (*Песня Земфиры из Цыганов* / *Старый муж, грозный муж...*): Pushkin wrote his narrative poem *Gypsies* in 1824; it was first published in full in 1827. It is a story of Moldavian gypsies, among whom Pushkin had stayed for a short time while he was stationed in Kishinyóv and from whom he seems to have picked up the original version of this song with its savage words and unusual staccato rhythm. A version of this song found its way, via Prosper Mérimée, into the libretto of the first act of Bizet's *Carmen*:

> Tra la, la, la; la, la, la, la,
> coupe-moi, brûle-moi,
> je ne te dirai rien!
> ....
> je brave tout, le feu,
> le fer et le ciel même!
> ....
> mon secret, je le garde
> et je le garde bien!
> ....

j'aime un autre et meurs
en disant que je l'aime!

In Pushkin's *Gypsies* the song is sung by the gypsy girl Zemfíra, who is tiring of her husband and preparing to abandon him for a younger man.

p. 63, *Shadows of the Past* (* * * / *Мой друг, забыты мной следы минувших лет...*): Written on 24th–25th August 1821 and first published in 1825. The addressee is unknown.

p. 64, *The Tenth Commandment* (*Десятая Заповедь* / *Добра чужого не желать...*): Written in 1821, but unpublished during Pushkin's lifetime. One of the more attractive local girls in Kishinyóv during Pushkin's posting there was a Jewess in her early twenties called Maria Eichfeldt (1798–1855). Although she was already married to a much older man, she lived on intimate terms with Pushkin's friend Nikolái Alexéyev. As Binyon explains, Pushkin "flirted with her in society, but refrained from pressing his advances further, as she was [his friend's] mistress". It seems to be this triangle that Pushkin had in mind here. The tenth of the Ten Commandments given by God to the Israelites was as follows: "Thou shalt not covet thy neighbour's house, thou shalt not covet thy neighbour's wife, nor his manservant, not his maidservant, not his ox, nor his ass, nor anything that is thy neighbour's." (Exodus 20,17)

p. 65, *For a Greek Girl* (*Гречанке* / *Ты рождена воспламенять...*): Written in 1822 and first published a year later. The poem is addressed to Kalipso Polikhroni (1802–27), for whom see *Alexander Pushkin's Life: Bessarabia 1820–23*, p. 182.

p. 66, *Something or Nothing?* (* * * / *Надеждой сладостной младенчески дыша...*): Written in 1823; unpublished in Pushkin's lifetime. The identity of the woman referred to at the end is uncertain.

p. 67, *Night* (*Ночь* / *Мой голос для тебя и ласковый и томный...*): Written on 26th October 1823, and first published in 1826. The first of a number of poems inspired by Amalia Riznić (1803–25), with whom Pushkin had an intense love affair in Odessa – see *Alexander Pushkin's Life: Odessa 1823–24*, p. 183.

p. 68, *Jealous Love* (* * * / *Простишь ли мне ревнивые мечты...*): Written on 11th November 1823; first published in 1824. Addressed again to Amalia Riznić – see note to the preceding poem.

p. 70, *Gullible Love* (* * * / *Как наше сердце своенравно!...*): An unfinished draft of this period, unpublished in Pushkin's lifetime. Probably also addressed to Amalia Riznić – see the two preceding poems and the relevant notes.

p. 71, *It's Finished* (* * * / *Все кончено: меж нами связи нет...*): Written in 1824; unpublished in Pushkin's lifetime. This poem apparently reflects one of the intermittent breakdowns in Pushkin's stormy relationship with Amalia Riznić – see the three preceding poems and the relevant notes. The final couplet is unrhymed, showing that Pushkin, deliberately or otherwise, left the poem unfinished.

p. 72, *Comparisons* (* * * / *Туманский прав, когда так верно вас...*): Written in 1824; unpublished in Pushkin's lifetime. The addressee is unknown. Vasíly Ivánovich Tumánsky (1800–60) was a minor poet, who worked in Odessa in the Governor-General's office and with whom Pushkin was on friendly terms during his stay there. None of Tumánsky's published poems, however, corresponds to the one Pushkin describes here.

p. 73, *A Storm* (*Буря* / *Ты видел деву на скале...*): Written in 1824; first published in 1827. Probably inspired by a seaside excursion with Elise Vorontsóva near Odessa – see *Alexander Pushkin's Life: Odessa 1823–24*, p. 183.

p. 77, *Proserpine* (*Прозерпина* / *Плещут волны Флегетона...*): Written on 26th August 1824, shortly after Pushkin's arrival in Mikháylovskoye from Odessa, and first published a year later. Pushkin's poem is an elaboration of a much slighter piece (*Les Déguisements de Vénus, Tableau XXVII*) by the French poet Évarist-Désiré de Parny (1753–1814). In working Parny's poem up, Pushkin has drawn directly on the description of the underworld in Virgil's *Aeneid*, Book VI. He has also turned the story into a parable of his own love affair in Odessa with Countess Elise Vorontsóva (1792–1880), who, like Proserpine, outranked her lover both in age and social position – see *Alexander Pushkin's Life: Odessa 1823–24*, p. 183. Proserpine in Roman mythology was the reluctant consort of Pluto, king of Hades and god of death. Phlegethon was one of the rivers of the underworld, as was Lēthē, the river of forgetfulness. *Ivory door*: according to Virgil (and Homer), dreams reach us from the underworld through two doors: one of horn, through which come dreams that prove true; and the other of ivory, the source of false dreams: Pushkin seems here to be hinting at his disappointment at the unhappy ending of his love affair with Elise Vorontsóva; his initial happiness had proved to be illusory.

p. 79, *The Rain-Quenched Day* (* * * / *Ненастный день потух; ненастной ночи мгла...*): Written, apparently, in autumn 1824, not long after Pushkin's arrival in Mikháylovskoye for the beginning of his exile, and expressing his thoughts of Elise Vorontsóva left behind in Odessa. Although the poem is ostensibly unfinished, Pushkin had it published in this form in 1826, suggesting that the broken, incoherent ending is deliberate.

p. 80, *The Desire for Fame* (*Желание Славы* / *Когда, любовию и негой упоенный...*): Completed in spring 1825, and published later that year. Another poem recalling Elise Vorontsóva – see *Alexander Pushkin's Life: Exile at Mikháylovskoye 1824–26*, p. 184.

p. 81, *Save Me, My Talisman...* (* * * / *Храни меня, мой талисман...*): Written in exile in 1825; unpublished in Pushkin's lifetime. The talisman – a ring – was given to Pushkin by Elise Vorontsóva; the bitter recollections in the last two stanzas refer to Amalia Riznić; for both see *Alexander Pushkin's Life: Odessa 1823–24*, pp. 183–184.

p. 82, *The Burned Letter* (*Сожженное Письмо* / *Прощай, письмо любви! прощай: она велела...*): Written in late 1824, and first published in 1826. Another poem referring to Elise Vorontsóva – see above – who corresponded secretly with Pushkin for a while after his departure for exile.

p. 83, *The Melancholy Moon* (* * * / *На небесах печальная луна...*): A rough draft, not published in Pushkin's lifetime. For Elvína see note on 'To Elvína' in Part I above.

p. 84, *Spanish Love Song* (* * * / *Ночной зефир...*): Written on 13th November 1824; first published in 1827 in a musical setting by Verstóvsky. *Guadalquivir*: the Guadalquivir is the chief river of Andalusia, which flows through Seville.

p. 85, *Liza* (* * * / *Лизе страшно полюбить...*): Written in 1824; unpublished in Pushkin's lifetime. It is not known who Liza was: she may be fictional. Diana in classical mythology was celebrated as a maiden goddess (of hunting, the moon, etc.), but she yielded to a secret passion for a handsome shepherd called Endymion.

p. 86, *Anna's Name Day* (* * * / *Хотя стишки на именины...*): Written in 1825 for the name day (3rd February) of Anna Nikoláyevna Vulf (1799–1857), eldest daughter of Pushkin's neighbour, Praskóvya Ósipova, by her first marriage – see *Alexander Pushkin's Life: Exile at Mikháylovskoye 1824–26* on p. 184. The name Anna comes from the Hebrew word for "grace".

p. 87, *A Confession* (*Признание* / *Я вас люблю, — хоть я бешусь...*): Written between late 1824 and 1826; unpublished in Pushkin's lifetime. Addressed to Alexándra (Alína) Ivánovna Ósipova (1808–64), step-daughter of Pushkin's neighbour, Praskóvya Ósipova – see *Alexander Pushkin's Life: Exile at Mikháylovskoye 1824–26* on p. 184. *Jealous torment*: the cause of Pushkin's jealousy was Alína's affection for her stepbrother Alexéy Nikoláyevich Vulf (1805–81), who was also often at Trigórskoye when not studying at university.

p. 89, *To Praskóvya Ósipova* (*П. А. Осиповой* / *Быть может, уж недолго мне...*): Written in Ósipova's album on 25th June 1825, reflecting Pushkin's plans, never fulfilled, to jump his detention and flee abroad. First published in 1829. For Praskóvya Ósipova (1781–1859), mistress of Trigórskoye, the neighbouring estate to Pushkin's, see *Alexander Pushkin's Life: Exile at Mikháylovskoye 1824–26* on p. 184.

p. 90, *To Rodzyánko* (*К Родзянке / Ты обещал о романтизме...*): A verse epistle written in late May or early June 1825; unpublished in Pushkin's lifetime. Arkády Gavrílovich Rodzyánko (1793–1846), a minor poet, had been a friend of Pushkin's in St Petersburg and was now living at Lubny in Ukraine. From Mikháylovskoye Pushkin started up a light-hearted correspondence with him, mainly about poetry, but also about Rodzyánko's current partner Anna Petróvna Kern (1800–79), a niece of Praskóvya Ósipova – see *Alexander Pushkin's Life: Exile at Mikháylovskoye 1824–26*, pp. 184–185. Rodzyánko's latest letter, instead of responding to Pushkin's comments about poetry, had dealt almost entirely with his relationship with Anna. Anna had been talking (whether seriously or just to tease Rodzyánko) of making up with her husband, in order to bear a legitimate family of children. Rodzyánko, it seems, would have preferred her to divorce him. Pushkin is here suggesting that Anna's relations with her husband and with Rodzyánko are not necessarily incompatible. (Soon after this, Anna visited her aunt at Trigórskoye and captivated Pushkin himself.)

p. 92, *To Anna Kern* (*К*** / Я помню чудное мгновенье...*): Written in June 1825; first published, without name of addressee, in 1827. For Anna Kern, see preceding note and *Alexander Pushkin's Life: Exile at Mikháylovskoye 1824–26*, pp. 184–185. Pushkin presented her with this verse as she was leaving Trigórskoye for Riga.

p. 93, *Sappho* (*Сафо / Счастливый юноша, ты всем меня пленил...*): Written in 1825 and published the following year. Sappho, the Greek poetess of Lesbos from the seventh century BC, was much admired in antiquity for her love poetry, but this survives today almost entirely in brief fragments. These three lines are not a translation, but an original composition by Pushkin in the style of a Sappho fragment.

p. 94, *On the Death of Amalia Riznić* (**** / Под небом голубым страны своей родной...*): Written on 29th July 1826, when news reached the exiled Pushkin of Amalia Riznić's death in Italy from consumption a year earlier. See *Alexander Pushkin's Life: Odessa 1823–24* and *The Decembrist Revolt 1825* on p. 183 and p. 185.

p. 97, *Cleopatra* (*Клеопатра / Чертог сиял. Гремели хором...*): Pushkin worked intermittently on this poem between 1824 and 1835, but never produced a definitive text; it was never published in his lifetime. This latest text, conjecturally compiled from Pushkin's notebooks, is the one he was preparing to incorporate in his unpublished short story 'Egyptian Nights', written within a couple of years of his death (see *The Queen of Spades and Other Stories* by Alexander Pushkin, published by Alma Classics in 2011). Cleopatra VII (68–30 BC) was the last queen of an independent Egypt, whose capital was Alexandria. Beautiful, sensual and ambitious, she was famous for her liaisons, both passionate and political, first with Julius Caesar and later with Mark Antony. The episode related here, certainly fictional, is derived from an anonymous set of Latin biographies of famous personalities that was once attributed to the late Roman historian Sextus Aurelius Victor (active in the later fourth century AD).

p. 100, *The Man I Was Before...* (* * * / *Каков я прежде был, таков и ныне я...*): Written in 1826, shortly after his return from exile to metropolitan life; apparently an unfinished fragment, but published by Pushkin in this form in 1832. The epigraph, which Pushkin translates as his first line, is the beginning of an elegy by the French poet André Chénier (1762–94), but the rest of the poem is Pushkin's own.

p. 101, *For Nanny* (*Няне / Подруга дней моих суровых...*): Written at the end of October 1826, a month and a half after Pushkin's return from exile; uncompleted and unpublished during his lifetime. The poem is addressed to Pushkin's beloved old nurse Arína Rodiónovna Yákovleva (1758–1828), who was his companion and housekeeper during exile at Mikháylovskoye.

p. 102, *A Riverbank by Night* (* * * / *Как счастлив я, когда могу покинуть...*): An apparently unfinished piece, written on 23rd November 1826 during a brief visit to Mikháylovskoye. Unpublished in Pushkin's lifetime. The poem describes a *rusalka*, a sinister Slavic water-nymph who lived at the bottom of rivers and lured young men to a watery death. Unusually, Pushkin composed the poem in unrhymed iambic pentameters.

p. 103, *The Winter Road* (*Зимняя Дорога / Сквозь волнистые туманы...*): Written during Pushkin's journey to the west of Russia in November–December 1826; first published in 1828. The addressee, Nina, is probably fictional.

p. 104, *A Correction* (*Ответ Ф. Т*** / Нет, не черкешенка она...*): Written at the end of 1826; first published in 1829. The subject is Sófya Fyódorovna Púshkina (1806–62) – see *Alexander Pushkin's Life: Rehabilitation 1826–31*, p. 186. Pushkin's poet friend Tumánsky had written a verse in Sófya's album comparing her to a Circassian girl and her eyes to agates; this is Pushkin's reply. Mount Kazbek is a high peak on the Georgian side of the Caucasus range.

p. 105, *The Unresponsive Rose* (*Соловей и Роза / В безмолвии садов, весной, во мгле ночей...*): Written in 1827 and first published that year.

p. 106, *For Yekaterína N. Ushakóva* (*Ек. Н. Ушаковой / Когда, бывало, в старину...*): An album verse written on 3rd April 1827; unpublished in Pushkin's lifetime. Yekaterína Nikoláyevna Ushakóva (1809–72), a friend of Pushkin's, was celebrating her eighteenth birthday; she apparently challenged Pushkin to compose a verse incorporating the folkloric incantation used to ward off evil spirits: "Amen, amen, begone!"

p. 107, *The Angel* (*Ангел / В дверях эдема ангел нежный...*): Written in 1827 and first published the following year.

p. 108, *The Talisman* (*Талисман / Там, где море вечно плещет...*): Written on 6th November 1827, and first published the following year. The poem is a reworking, in a more exotic setting, of the talisman theme, for which see 'Save Me, My Talisman...' in Part IV above and its note.

p. 110, *Trinity* (*Кж. Урусовой / Не веровал я троице доныне...*): Dating from 1827; Pushkin's authorship is unconfirmed, but highly plausible. The epigram is based on a similar verse of 1759 by Voltaire, one of Pushkin's favourite authors:

Oui, j'en conviens, chez moi la Trinité
jusqu'à présent n'avait du tout fortune;
mais j'aperçois les trois grâces en une:
vous confondez mon incrédulité.

Princess Sófya Alexándrovna Urúsova (1804–89) was a renowned beauty, admired by Pushkin at this time, and the verse was doubtless destined for her album. The Princess is, however, addressed with the formal pronoun *vy*, suggesting that the poet's relations with her were not intimate. In Greco-Roman mythology the three Graces were sister goddesses personifying charm, grace and beauty.

p. 111, *St Petersburg* (* * * / *Город пышный, город бедный...*): Written in 1828; first published in 1829. Pushkin's metre is eight lines of trochaic tetrameters, alternately rhymed. The final two lines are said to refer to Annette Olénina – see next note.

p. 112, *Songs of Georgia* (* * * / *Не пой, красавица, при мне...*): Written on 12th June 1828; first published in 1829. The poem is addressed to Anna ("Annette") Alexéyevna Olénina (1808–88), whom Pushkin was courting this year – see *Alexander Pushkin's Life: Rehabilitation 1826–31*, p. 186. The identity of the "poor young lass" in "a far-off land" is uncertain. Pushkin seems to be referring to a girl he met during his time in the Caucasus in 1820. The composer Glinka, who taught Annette singing, set the words to a Georgian melody.

p. 113, *Dedication of* Poltava (*Полтава – Посвящение / Тебе — но голос музы тёмной...*): This dedication was written on 27th October 1828 and published the following year with Pushkin's narrative poem *Poltava*, whose heroine Pushkin named María. The addressee is probably María Nikoláyevna Volkónskaya (née Rayévskaya, 1805–63) now in self-imposed exile in Siberia – see *Alexander Pushkin's Life: Travels in the South 1820*, p. 181, and *Rehabilitation 1826–31*, p. 186.

p. 114, *A Portrait* (*Портрет / С своей пылающей душой...*): Written in 1828 and first published in the following year. The poem describes Agraféna Fyódorovna Zakrévskaya (1800–79), wife of a senior government figure, who was admired by Pushkin for her beauty and notorious in St Petersburg society for her unconventional lifestyle and extravagant and unpredictable behaviour.

p. 115, *Disfavour* (* * * / *Когда твои младые лета...*): Written in 1829 and first published the following year. Usually assumed to refer to Agraféna Zakrévskaya – see preceding note.

p. 116, *A Flower* (*Цветок / Цветок засохший, безуханный...*): Written in 1828 and first published the following year.

p. 117, *Message from Georgia* (* * * / *На холмах Грузии лежит ночная мгла...*): Adapted from a longer draft written in Georgia during Pushkin's visit to the Caucasus in 1829; first published in 1831. In its final form apparently addressed to Natálya Nikoláyevna Goncharóva (1812–63), Pushkin's future wife, whom he had begun to court that spring in Moscow at the start of his journey southwards. The Arágva is a river of Georgia, rising on the southern slopes of the Caucasus.

p. 118, *For a Kalmyk Girl* (*Калмычке / Прощай, любезная калмычка!...*): Dated by Pushkin 22nd May 1829, and written during his visit to the Caucasus that year; first published in 1830. The Kalmyks (or Kalmuks) were a widely dispersed nomadic people of Mongolian extraction, one branch of which roamed the area to the west and north-west of the Caspian Sea. *De Vigny's books*: Pushkin refers specifically to *Cinq Mars*, a historical novel by the French writer Alfred de Vigny (1797–1863), published in 1826, of which he had a low opinion. *Arias by Rossini*: Pushkin mentions 'Ma dov'è', an aria, written for male voice, from Act I, Sc. 9, of Rossini's opera *La donna del lago* (1819).

p. 119, *2nd November* (* * * (*2 ноября*) / *Зима. Что делать нам в деревне? Я встречаю...*): Later in 1829, on his way back from the Caucasus via Moscow, Pushkin stopped off at the estate of some friends between Moscow and St Petersburg. He dated this poem "2nd November" during his stay there. It was first published in 1830, the apparently uncompleted ending being deliberate. Although Pushkin presents the poem as a diary entry, it is clear from his notes that some at least of the details (e.g. the two visiting sisters) are fantasy.

p. 121, *Winter Morning* (*Зимнее Утро / Мороз и солнце; день чудесный!*): Written on 3rd November 1829, the day after the date of the preceding poem; first published in 1830. Again the details are more imagined than autobiographical.

p. 122, *Escape* (* * * / *Поедем, я готов; куда бы вы, друзья...*): Written on 23rd December 1829; its apparently unfinished ending is deliberate: it was first published in this form the following year. The poem reflects a low point in his courtship of Natálya Goncharóva – see *Alexander Pushkin's Life: Rehabilitation 1826–31*, p. 186.

p. 123, *I Loved You* (* * * / *Я вас любил: любовь еще, быть может...*): Written in 1829; first published the following year. Famous though this poem is, no one has convincingly identified the woman to whom it is addressed. The traditional ascription to Annette Olénina is implausible, as her rejection of Pushkin's courtship in September of that year left him bitter towards the whole family. Unusually for Pushkin's deeply felt love poems, she is addressed with the formal pronoun *vy*, suggesting either that Pushkin was never on intimate terms with her, or that he is now deliberately distancing himself.

p. 124, *My Autograph* (* * * / *Что в имени тебе моем?...*): Written in 1829 and inscribed on 5th January 1830 in the album of Karolina Sobańska – see *Alexander Pushkin's Life: Rehabilitation 1826–31*, p. 187. The verse was published later the same year.

p. 125, *Madonna* (*Мадона* / *Не множеством картин старинных мастеров...*): Written on 8th July 1830; first published the following year. The sonnet is addressed to Natálya Goncharóva, Pushkin's future wife. On 30th July 1830 Pushkin wrote in a letter from St Petersburg to his fiancée in Moscow: "*Les belles dames me demandent à voir votre portrait, et ne me pardonnent pas de ne pas l'avoir. Je me console en passant des heures entières devant une madone blonde qui vous ressemble comme deux gouttes d'eau, et que j'aurais achetée, si elle ne coûtait pas 40,000 roubles.*" ["The ladies keep asking me if they can see your portrait and don't forgive me for not having it. For consolation I spend hours on end gazing at a blonde Madonna, which is as like you as one drop of water's like another and which I'd have bought if it didn't cost 40,000 roubles." (French)] Commentators have identified the painting as a copy of Raphael's "Bridgewater Madonna", the original of which is now on loan to the National Gallery of Scotland in Edinburgh. Though the original features no palm tree, the copyist had apparently added a view of a tree through a window in the background of the picture.

p. 126, *Burden of the Past* (* * * / *Когда в объятия мои...*): Though possibly a reworking of an earlier draft, this version dates from 1830 and is apparently addressed to Natálya Goncharóva, Pushkin's future wife. It was unpublished during Pushkin's lifetime.

p.   127, *Rhyme* (*Рифма / Эхо, бессонная нимфа, скиталась по брегу Пенея...*): Written at Bóldino on 10th October 1830; first published in 1832. No doubt to match the subject matter drawn from classical mythology, Pushkin has used here a classical metre: elegiac couplets – i.e. alternating dactylic hexameters and pentameters – in the style of much of the *Greek Anthology* and of Roman lyric poets such as Ovid. Thus, ironically, Pushkin's poem commemorating rhyme is expressed in the forms and traditions of Greco-Roman poetry and so is itself unrhymed. Naiads were nymphs of springs, rivers and lakes.

p.   128, *The Page*, or *At the Age of Fifteen* (*Паж, или Пятнадцатый Год / Пятнадцать лет мне скоро минет...*): Written at Bóldino on 7th October 1830; unpublished in Pushkin's lifetime. The epigraph and the mention of "my countess from the south of Spain" in the penultimate line make it clear that Pushkin had in mind Chérubin/ Cherubino, the amorous young page in Beaumarchais's play *Le Mariage de Figaro* and Mozart's *Le nozze di Figaro*, both set in Seville. Mozart and Beaumarchais were both in Pushkin's thoughts at this time, as he was writing his Little Tragedy *Mozart and Salieri* (in which Beaumarchais is mentioned) in Bóldino this same October. There is evidence from Pushkin's notebooks that he also had in view the teenage brother of one of his St Petersburg friends, who had just graduated from the imperial Corps of Pages and joined the Life Guards.

p.   130, *Farewell* (*Прощание / В последний раз твой образ милый...*): Written in Bóldino on 5th October 1830; first published in a musical setting a year or so later. Addressed in thought to Elise Vorontsóva, whom Pushkin had loved in Odessa – see *Alexander Pushkin's Life: Odessa 1823–24* on p. 183.

p.   131, *Invocation* (*Заклинание / О, если правда, что в ночи...*): Written at Bóldino on 17th October 1830; unpublished in Pushkin's lifetime. The poem is almost certainly addressed to the memory of Amalia Riznić – for whom see *Alexander Pushkin's Life* p. 183. Leila is the name of the heroine of Byron's *The Giaour*, who, having been put to death for infidelity, appeared to her lover from beyond the grave. *Why they killed the friend I miss*: there were rumours that Amalia had been murdered at the behest of her husband, who resented her unfaithfulness and wished to remarry more advantageously; the rumours were probably false – she almost certainly died of consumption – but Pushkin was tempted to believe them.

p.   132, *The Promise* (* * * / *Для берегов отчизны дальной...*): Written at Bóldino on 27th November 1830; unpublished in Pushkin's lifetime.

The poem is addressed to the memory of Amalia Riznić, for whom see note above. *Your dear homeland*: though born in Vienna, Amalia had regarded the Italian port of Trieste, her husband's city, as her home since her marriage and returned there when she left Odessa.

p. 133, *Serenade to Inesilla* (* * * / *Я здесь, Инезилья...*): Written at Bóldino on 9th October 1830; first published in 1834 as the lyrics to a song by Glinka. Pushkin possibly intended it for a Spanish song for his Little Tragedy *The Stone Guest*, which he was composing at Bóldino and which he completed there at the beginning of November; in the end, though, *The Stone Guest* was set in Madrid, not Seville.

p. 134, *Scottish Girl's Song* (*Песня Шотландки, из Пиры во время чумы / Было время, процветала...*): Written for inclusion in Pushkin's Little Tragedy *A Feast during the Plague*, which he completed at Bóldino on 6th November 1830; it was first published in 1832. The play was suggested to Pushkin by the deadly cholera epidemic then raging across Russia. Though the play is set in London during the plague of 1665, this song portrays the effect of the plague on a rural community in Scotland.

p. 139, *A Different Kind of Love* (* * * / *Нет, я не дорожу мятежным наслажденьем...*): Written probably in 1831; unpublished in Pushkin's lifetime. Addressed to his wife Natálya Púshkina (née Goncharóva).

p. 140, *Second Meeting* (*В Альбом Кж. А. Д. Абамелек / Когда-то (помню с умиленьем)...*): Written on 9th April 1832; unpublished in Pushkin's lifetime. A verse for the album of Princess Anna Davýdovna Abamelék (1814–89), who (it seems) had as a baby been brought on a visit to the imperial Lycée while Pushkin was still a pupil there. By 1832 she was already an acclaimed beauty and was soon to be appointed a maid-of-honour to the Empress. She became famous as a poet and translator, translating works by Pushkin and other Russian writers into French. Pushkin uses the formal pronoun *vy* in addressing the Princess in this verse.

p. 141, *Memory of Moscow* (*В Альбом / Гонимый рока самовластьем...*): Written on 27th October 1832; unpublished in Pushkin's lifetime. The addressee is unknown. Pushkin uses the formal pronoun *vy* for the addressee in this verse. Moscow was Pushkin's home till the age of twelve, and he always retained an affection for the city.

p. 142, *Name-Day Greeting* (*В Альбом / Долго сих листов заветных...*): Written probably in 1832; unpublished in Pushkin's lifetime. The addressee is not known.

p. 143, *A Beautiful Woman* (*Красавица / Всё в ней гармония, всё диво...*): Another album verse, written on 16th May 1832 for Countess Yeléna Mikháylovna Zavadóvskaya (1807–74). First published in 1834.

p. 144, *Detachment* (*К *** / Нет, нет, не должен я, не смею, не могу...*): Written in 1832; unpublished in Pushkin's lifetime. Thought to be addressed to Countess Nadézhda Lvovna Sollogúb (1815–1903). The translator has shortened Pushkin's iambic hexameter lines to tetrameters.

p. 145, *The Baron's Return* (*Воевода / Поздно ночью из похода...*): Written on 28th October 1833 and first published as a "Polish ballad" in 1834. The poem is a free translation of a ballad by the Polish poet Adam Mickiewicz.

p. 148, *Beauty's Power* (* * * / Я думал, сердце позабыло...*): Written during a visit to Mikháylovskoye in 1835 as the reworking of a draft from four years earlier; unpublished in Pushkin's lifetime. It is not known to whom Pushkin was referring in this poem.

p. 149, *Charming Lad* (*Подражание Арабскому / Отрок милый, отрок нежный...*): Written in 1835; unpublished in Pushkin's lifetime. Despite Pushkin's title ('After the Arabic'), no Arabic original or model has been identified, though the core metaphor in the last couplet has a precedent in the *Gulistan* of the thirteenth-century Persian poet Saadi. It is likely that, as in some other cases, Pushkin presented his own work as a translation or adaptation of a foreign text in order to forestall an adverse reaction from the censorship or public opinion.

p. 150, *Fragment from Anacreon* (*Отрывок из Анакреона / Узнают коней ретивых...*): Written on 6th January 1835; unpublished during Pushkin's lifetime. He seems to have intended the verse for incorporation in his unfinished short story known as *A Tale from Roman Life* (see *The Queen of Spades and Other Stories* by Alexander Pushkin, published by Alma Classics in 2011). Anacreon was a Greek lyric poet who flourished in the late sixth century BC. His work was very popular in the ancient world and much imitated. The verse translated by Pushkin is probably by a later imitator, since the Parthians here mentioned (a race originally from north-eastern Iran) did not impinge on the Greek world till much later. Pushkin would have worked from a French or earlier Russian version of the poem, as he did not know Greek.

p. 151, *Worldweariness* (* * * / Пора, мой друг, пора! покоя сердце просит...*): Probably written in June 1834, when Pushkin was trying unsuccessfully to get leave to go away into the country. It was unpublished in Pushkin's lifetime, and seems from his notes to be unfinished. It is addressed to Pushkin's wife Natálya.

Extra Material

on

Alexander Pushkin's

Love Poems

Alexander Pushkin's Life

Alexánder Sergéyevich Pushkin was born in Moscow in 1799. He came of an ancient, but largely undistinguished aristocratic line. Perhaps his most famous ancestor – and the one of whom Pushkin was most proud – was his mother's grandfather, Abrám Petróvich Gannibál (*c.*1693–1781), who was an African, most probably from Ethiopia or Cameroon. Kidnapped as a young boy, he was sold as a slave in Constantinople and sent as a gift to Tsar Peter the Great. Peter took a liking to the boy and in 1707 stood godfather to him at his christening (hence his patronymic Petróvich, "son of Peter"). Peter sent him abroad as a young man to study fortification and military mining. After seven years in France he was recalled to Russia, where he followed a career as a military engineer. Peter's daughter, the Empress Elizabeth, made him a general, and he eventually died in retirement well into his eighties on one of the estates granted him by the crown.

Family, Birth and Childhood

Pushkin had an older sister, Olga, and a younger brother, Lev. His parents did not show him much affection as a child, and he was left to the care of his grandmother and servants, including a nurse of whom he became very fond. As was usual in those days, his early schooling was received at home, mostly from French tutors and in the French language. His father possessed a large collection of books, especially of French literature, and one service he did his son was to give him free run of this library, of which the young Pushkin made precocious use.

In 1811, at the age of twelve, Pushkin was sent by his parents to St Petersburg to be educated at the new Lyceum (Lycée), a boarding school that the Emperor Alexander I had just established in a wing of his summer palace at Tsárskoye Seló to prepare the sons of noblemen for careers in the government service. Pushkin spent six happy years there, studying (his curriculum included Russian, French, Latin, German, state economy and finance, scripture, logic, moral philosophy, law, history, geography, statistics and mathematics), socializing with teachers and fellow students, and relaxing in the palace park. To the end of his life he remained deeply attached to his memories and friends from those years. In 1817 he graduated with a junior rank in the civil service, and was attached to the

School 1811–17

Ministry of Foreign Affairs, with duties that he was allowed to interpret as minimal.

While still at the Lycée, Pushkin had already started writing poetry, some of which had attracted the admiration of leading Russian literary figures of the time. This output included love poems addressed to living women that he met around the school and the palace grounds – e.g. older sisters of classmates ('To the Lovely Girl Who Took Snuff') or teachers' guests ('To a Young Widow'). Some that referred to real people were more in the nature of schoolboy pranks ('For Delivery to the Bábolovsky Palace'; 'Notice on the Infirmary Wall'). Other love poems were imitations of French classical and pastoral verse, fictional love tales or expressions of a schoolboy's amatory imagination.

St Petersburg
1817–20

Pushkin spent the next three years in St Petersburg living a life of pleasure and dissipation, such as he describes in 'To Shcherbínin'. He loved the company of friends, dinners, drinking parties, cards, the theatre – and particularly women. He took an interest in radical politics. And he continued to write poetry – mostly lyric verses and epigrams on personal, amatory or political subjects – often light and ribald, but always crisply, lucidly and euphoniously expressed. Some of these verses, even unpublished, gained wide currency in St Petersburg and attracted the unfavourable notice of the authorities.

It was probably only now that Pushkin had his first real sexual experiences, largely in the company of St Petersburg courtesans; he refers to a number of them in his verses of this period, notably Olga Masson, the cross-dressing Yelizavéta Schott-Schedel ('Recovery') and others whom he disguised behind names from classical poetry such as Dorída. His fondness for the theatre generated clever epigrams on leading actresses ('In Sosnítskaya's Album'), sometimes causing offence he had trouble making amends for ('Aimed at Kólosova'; 'To Katénin'). As a lively and witty young aristocrat of literary abilities and social and political interests, he also circulated in the distinguished St Petersburg salons of such women as Princess Yevdókiya Golítsyna; he repaid her and other society hostesses and friends for their patronage and hospitality with witty, elegant and complimentary verses, often inscribed in their visitors' albums ('Yelizavéta Ogaryóva'; 'Madrigal for M—'; 'To A. B—'; 'To Catherine Bakúnina').

Pushkin's major literary achievement of this period was *Ruslan and Lyudmila*, a light-hearted epic fairy tale in six cantos, completed in the early months of 1820. Before *Ruslan and Lyudmila* could be published, however, the Emperor Alexander I finally lost patience with the subversiveness of some of Pushkin's poetry and determined to remove him from the capital. He first considered exiling Pushkin to Siberia or the White Sea; but at the intercession of high-placed friends of Pushkin's the proposed sentence was commuted to a posting to the south of Russia. Even so, some supposed friends hurt and infuriated Pushkin by disowning him and even spreading exaggerated rumours about his disgrace. Pushkin expressed his shock and bitterness over these events in his Epilogue to *Ruslan and Lyudmila*, written only a few weeks after his departure from St Petersburg. Meanwhile, the main work was being published in the capital in Pushkin's absence, under the supervision of his friends; it was enthusiastically received by the public.

Pushkin was detailed to report to Lieutenant-General Iván Inzóv (1768–1845), who was at the time Commissioner for the Protection for Foreign Colonists in Southern Russia based at Yekaterinosláv (now Dnepropetróvsk) on the lower Dnieper. Inzóv gave him a friendly welcome, but little work to do, and before long Pushkin caught a fever from bathing in the river and was confined to bed in his poor lodgings. He was rescued by General Nikolái Rayévsky, a soldier who had distinguished himself in the war of 1812 against Napoleon. Rayévsky was travelling through Yekaterinosláv with his younger son (also called Nikolái), his two youngest daughters María and Sófya, Maria's Circassian-born companion Anna Giréy, a personal physician and other attendants; they were on their way to join the elder son Alexándr, who was taking a cure at the mineral springs in the Caucasus. General Rayévsky generously invited Pushkin to join them; and Inzóv gave him leave.

Travels in the South 1820

The party arrived in Pyatigórsk, in the northern foothills of the Caucasus, in June. Pushkin, along with his hosts, benefited from the waters and was soon well again. He accompanied the Rayévskys on long trips into the surrounding country, where he enjoyed the mountain scenery and observed the way of life of the local Circassian and Chechen tribes. In early August they set off westwards to join the rest of the Rayévsky family (the General's wife and two older daughters) at Gurzúf on the Crimean coast, where they had the use of a villa near the shore.

Pushkin enjoyed his Crimean stay – the majestic coastal scenery, the southern climate, the exotic Tatar ambience and the new experience of living in the midst of a harmonious, hospitable and intelligent family. Pushkin also fell in love with Yekaterína, the General's eldest daughter, whom he had met previously in St Petersburg. Yekaterína, who on their arrival in Gurzúf was still suffering from a serious chest infection, was the inspiration for several of Pushkin's poems now and later ('A Sick Girl'; 'A Nereïd'; 'Crimean Venus'). Yekaterína recovered from her illness, but she never reciprocated Pushkin's affections. Over the same period Pushkin also developed a fondness for

Yekaterína's younger sister María and perhaps for the companion Anna Giréy.

Before leaving the Crimea Pushkin travelled with the Rayévskys through the coastal mountains and inland to Bakhchisaráy, an oriental town which had till forty years before been the capital of the Tatar khans of the Crimea and where the khans' palace still stood (and stands). Pushkin later commemorated his visit to Bakhchisaráy in his narrative poem *The Fountain of Bakhchisaray* and in the lyric 'To the Fountain in the Palace of Bakhchisaráy'.

After a month in the Crimea it was time for the party to return to the mainland. During the summer General Inzóv had been transferred from Yekaterinosláv to be governor of Bessarabia (the northern slice of Moldavia, which Russia had annexed from Turkey only eight years previously). His new headquarters was in Kishinyóv (today, Chişinău), the chief town of Bessarabia. So it was to Kishinyóv that Pushkin went back to duty in September 1820. Pushkin was based there till 1823, though with several periods of leave, including a lengthy absence during the winter of 1820–21 in the Ukraine, at Kámenka on the lower Dnieper and in Kiev, once more in the company of the Rayévskys. Kámenka was the estate of the Davýdov family; and there Pushkin had a short-lived affair with the promiscuous French-born lady of the house, Aglaë Davýdova ('For a Flirt').

Bessarabia 1820–23

Kishinyóv was still, apart from recently arrived Russian officials and soldiers, a raw near-eastern town, with few buildings of stone or brick, populated by Moldavians and other Balkan nationalities. Despite the contrast with St Petersburg, Pushkin still passed a lot of his time in a similar lifestyle of camaraderie, drinking, gambling, womanizing and quarrelling, with little official work. One woman he consorted with at this period was Kalipso Polikhroni, a young Greek refugee from Turkey, who attracted the interest of Pushkin and others by claiming (quite implausibly) to have associated with Lord Byron in Constantinople ('To a Greek Girl'). Pushkin also, as in the Caucasus and Crimea, took a close interest in the indigenous cultures, visiting local fairs and living for a few days with a band of Moldavian gypsies, an experience on which he later drew in his narrative poem *Gypsies*.

Just before his departure from Kishinyóv in 1823, Pushkin composed the first few stanzas of his greatest work, the novel in verse *Eugene Onegin*.

Odessa 1823–24

In the summer of 1823, through the influence of his friends in St Petersburg, Pushkin was posted to work for Count Mikhaíl Vorontsóv, who had just been appointed Governor General of the newly Russianized region south of the Ukraine. Vorontsóv's headquarters were to be in Odessa, the port city on the Black Sea founded by Catherine the Great thirty years previously. Despite its newness Odessa was a far more lively, cosmopolitan and cultured place than Kishinyóv, and Pushkin was pleased with the change. He only remained in Odessa for a year, but during this time he experienced two of the most intense love affairs of his life, which left a deep imprint on his poetic imagination.

The first of these affairs was with Amalia Riznić (née Ripp), a girl of Austro-Italian parentage from Vienna. When she was still in her teens her father contracted a marriage for her with Jovan Riznić, a Croatian businessman from Trieste over twice her age. Already wealthy, Riznić brought his attractive young wife, still only twenty, to Odessa in the spring of 1823. The marriage was a loveless one, at least on her part, and the free-living Amalia soon surrounded herself with a swarm of young admirers, Pushkin among them. Pushkin describes a visit to Odessa's opera house:

> And what of that box where a businessman's young wife was radiating beauty, so vain, so yielding, encircled by a crowd of devotees? She heard the aria, and didn't hear it; she heard, and didn't hear, their pleas, their banter mingled half-and-half with flattery... The husband? He dozed on at the back behind her, half woke to shout "encore" – then yawned and snored again.
>
> *(Onegin's Journey 28)*

Pushkin's relationship with Amalia was an on-off affair of infatuation, jealousy, self-deception, estrangement and reconciliation ('Night'; 'Jealous Love'; 'Gullible Love'; 'It's Finished'). During her time in Odessa Amalia developed a consumptive illness, which got progressively worse; in the spring of 1824 her husband decided on medical advice to send her back to Trieste so that she could benefit from the Italian climate. The parting, recalled by Pushkin years later, was an emotional and painful one. After she had left Odessa, however, Pushkin came to believe that she had played him false with a rival; it left bitter memories (the last two stanzas of 'Save Me, My Talisman').

Pushkin did not get on well with his chief in Odessa, Count Vorontsóv, partly because of temperamental differences and partly because Pushkin objected to the work Vorontsóv expected him to do; but an additional factor was that, following an encounter one day on the beach, Pushkin, still smarting from his disappointment over Amalia Riznić, fell passionately in love with the Countess, Yelizavéta (Elise) Vorontsóva, an attractive woman of Polish descent. The Countess failed to discourage

Pushkin's advances – her husband had mistresses of his own – and they used to meet at a seaside villa with a bathing place beneath the cliffs ('A Storm').

Vorontsóv tried hard to get Pushkin transferred elsewhere; and Pushkin for his part became so unhappy with his position on the Count's staff that he tried to resign and even contemplated escaping overseas. But before matters came to a head the police intercepted a letter from Pushkin to a friend in which he spoke approvingly of the atheistic views of an Englishman he had met in the city. The authorities in St Petersburg now finally lost patience with Pushkin: he was dismissed from the service and sent to indefinite banishment on his mother's country estate of Mikháylovskoye in the west of Russia. This abrupt loss of freedom came as a great shock to Pushkin. It also put an end to his brief affair with the Countess: they had an emotional parting by night in an Odessa garden, where she gave him as a keepsake an inscribed ring that he continued to treasure for long afterwards ('Save Me, My Talisman'; 'The Talisman'). Pushkin left Odessa for Mikháylovskoye on 1st August 1824.

Exile at Mikháylovskoye 1824–26

Pushkin spent more than two years under police surveillance at Mikháylovskoye. The enforced leisure gave him a lot of time for writing: he completed *Gypsies*; added further chapters to *Eugene Onegin*; and composed his historical drama *Boris Godunov* as well as many shorter works. Pushkin's lyrics from this time initially reflected his nostalgia for the South and for his curtailed affair with Elise Vorontsóva, with whom for a time he maintained a covert correspondence ('The Rain-Quenched Day'; 'The Desire for Fame'; 'The Burned Letter'). But in due course he developed more local interests.

A neighbouring estate to Mikháylovskoye was Trigórskoye, occupied by Praskóvya Ósipova, a twice-widowed forty-three-year-old, with her large family, including daughters by both her first husband Nikolái Vulf and her second husband Iván Ósipov, plus a stepdaughter, Ósipov's child by a previous marriage. She was also visited by various nieces. Although Pushkin at first looked down on his neighbours as dull, provincial and uncultivated compared with the high society of St Petersburg and Odessa, he eventually warmed towards them. Pushkin had relationships, superficial or intense, with several of the girls at different times. This collection includes poems to the eldest daughter Anna Vulf ('Anna's Name Day') and to the stepdaughter Alína Ósipova ('A Confession'). Pushkin had particularly warm feelings towards the mother, who became something of a mother figure to him too ('For Praskóvya Ósipova').

In 1819 Pushkin had briefly met one niece of Ósipova's, another Anna, in St Petersburg, and had been bowled over by her. Anna had married the much older General Kern. She was now estranged from him and had been living with a friend of Pushkin's in the Ukraine ('To Rodzyánko'). Parting in turn from him, she came in June 1825 to visit her aunt at Trigórskoye. Pushkin once again fell for her ('To Anna Kern'), but their intimacy was forestalled by Ósipova, who took her niece off the same month to be reconciled, temporarily, to her husband in Riga.

In November 1825 Alexander I died unexpectedly. He left no children, and there was initially confusion over the succession. In December some liberally minded members of the army and the intelligentsia (subsequently known as the Decembrists) seized the opportunity to attempt a coup d'état. This was put down by the new Emperor Nicholas I, a younger brother of Alexander's. Among the conspirators were several old friends of Pushkin; and he might well have joined them had he been at liberty. As it was, the leading conspirators were executed, and many of the rest were sent to Siberia for long spells of hard labour and exile. Pushkin feared that he too might be punished. In June 1826, at about the same time as he heard news of the executions, Pushkin received a further shock, learning belatedly of the death of Amalia Riznić: she had never recovered from her chest ailment and had died of it a year previously in Trieste. Pushkin recorded in verse his numbed reaction ('On the Death of Amalia Riznić'). *The Decembrist Revolt 1825*

In September Pushkin was suddenly summoned to Moscow to see the new emperor. Nicholas surprised Pushkin by offering him his freedom, and Pushkin assured Nicholas of his future good conduct. Pushkin complained that he had difficulty in making money from his writing because of the censorship, and Nicholas undertook to oversee Pushkin's work personally. In practice, however, the Emperor delegated the task to the Chief of the Secret Police, and, despite occasional interventions from Nicholas, Pushkin continued to have difficulty with the censors. *Rehabilitation 1826–31*

Pushkin immediately threw himself back into metropolitan life and resumed his old habits ('The Man I Was Before'), though he still remembered with regret his old nurse, who had been his housekeeper and confidante during his exile in Mikháylovskoye and to whom he remained fondly attached ('For Nanny'). In the November he made a short return trip to Mikháylovskoye to sort out his affairs there, a trip that generated more poetry ('A Riverbank by Night'; 'A Winter Road'). His resumed social life in Moscow, and later in St Petersburg, entailed the composition of fresh album verses ('For Yekaterína Ushakóva'; 'Trinity') and other poems addressed to friends in high society ('A Portrait'; 'Disfavour'). After a few months in Moscow Pushkin returned to St Petersburg, where he spent most of his time in the coming years, though he continued periodically to visit Moscow, call at the family's estates and stay with friends in the country ('2nd November'; 'Winter Morning').

At the end of 1826, before he left Moscow, Pushkin had had a final meeting with María Rayévskaya, of whom he had remained fond since their time together in the Caucasus and Crimea in 1820 and subsequent meetings in Kiev and Odessa. In 1825 Maria had married Prince Sergéi Volkónsky, a general seventeen years her senior; Volkónsky, it turned out, was among the Decembrist conspirators and was subsequently sentenced to twenty years of penal labour and lifelong exile in Siberia for his part in the abortive uprising. Against the wishes of her family and of the Emperor, María had insisted on joining her husband in exile, and she was on her way through Moscow to Siberia when Pushkin met her. Her loyalty made a deep impression on him. When in 1828 Pushkin wrote his historical novella in verse *Poltava*, whose heroine, named "María" by Pushkin, left her parents to live with a man much older than herself who then led an uprising against Tsar Peter I – it seems to be this María that Pushkin addressed in the poem's dedication.

In 1829 Pushkin made his only visit abroad: after revisiting the Caucasus and observing the local people ('For a Kalmyk Girl'), he followed the Russian army on a campaign into north-eastern Turkey.

During the late 1820s Pushkin made several attempts to find a wife, with a view to settling down. Soon after his arrival in Moscow in 1826 he fell in love with a distant cousin, Sófya Púshkina ('A Correction'); he proposed to her, but was refused. After several other unsuccessful liaisons he cultivated a relationship during 1828 with Annette Olénina, daughter of the President of the Academy of Arts and Director of the Imperial Public Library ('St Petersburg'); but again his proposal was rejected – perhaps not surprisingly in view of Pushkin's evidently divided affections ('Songs of Georgia'). In 1829 he met Natálya Goncharóva, an exceptionally attractive, but shy and inexperienced sixteen-year-old from an impoverished noble family. He wrote to her fondly during his visit to the Caucasus in 1829 ('Message from Georgia'). But once again his proposal was received initially with coldness, and Pushkin was tempted to abandon the suit ('Escape'). He did indeed ask the authorities for permission to travel abroad, but was turned down. In April 1830, however, to Pushkin's relief and delight, he and Natálya were eventually engaged ('Madonna'; 'Legacy of the Past'), and early in 1831 they were married.

Earlier in 1830, while still unsure whether his proposal to Natálya Goncharóva would be accepted, Pushkin cultivated the friendship in St Petersburg of a formidable Polish noblewoman, Karolina Sobańska, whom he had met previously in Kiev, Odessa and St Petersburg ('My Autograph'). Sobańska was famous for her beauty and for her social and political connexions in Russia. It was from Sobańska, an old acquaintance of Jovan and Amalia Riznić and Jovan Riznić's sister-in-law since his second marriage, that Pushkin would have gathered information about the circumstances of Amalia's departure from Odessa that reconciled him to her memory.

That autumn Pushkin visited the family estate of Bóldino, some 600 kilometres east of Moscow, which his father had agreed to settle on him. He found himself marooned there for a couple of months by a cholera epidemic, and he used the spare time to write. This was when he virtually completed *Onegin* and composed a number of other works; these included *A Feast during the Plague*, one of his *Little Tragedies*, the subject of which was suggested by the cholera epidemic then raging, and a wide range of love lyrics (including the last seven in Part V). Pushkin was fully aware at this time of the change in lifestyle, and indeed in attitude to other women, that marriage would call for. It was a change that he analysed in *The Stone Guest*, another of his *Little Tragedies*, based on the *Don Juan* legend. He took the opportunity of his enforced leisure at Bóldino to wish an imaginary goodbye to a number of his earlier loves, including Elise Vorontsóva and the deceased Amalia Riznić ('Farewell'; 'The Promise').

After his marriage Pushkin continued to live in St Petersburg and its environs, participating (with increasing reluctance) in the social life of the capital and continuing to entertain hostesses and other acquaintances with album verses ('Second Meeting'; 'Memory of Moscow'; 'Name-Day Greeting'). During these years he composed much less amatory verse than previously, and such love poetry as he did write is notably more restrained ('A Beautiful Woman'; 'Detachment'; 'Beauty's Power').

The Final Years 1831–37

The 1830s were not on the whole happy years for Pushkin. His marriage, it is true, was more successful than might have been expected. An unusually intimate account of the couple's sexual relationship early on is given in 'Different Kinds of Love'. Natálya, however, was thirteen years Pushkin's junior; her remarkable beauty and susceptibility to admiration constantly exposed her to the attentions of other men; she showed more liking for society and its entertainments than for intellectual or artistic pursuits or for household management; her fashionable tastes and social aspirations incurred outlays that the pair could ill afford; and she took little interest in her husband's writing. Nonetheless, despite all this they seem to have remained a loyal and loving couple; Natálya bore Pushkin four children in less than six years of marriage; and she showed real anguish at his untimely death.

But there were other difficulties. Pushkin, though short of money himself and with a costly family of his own to maintain, was often called upon to help out his parents, his brother and sister and his in-laws, and so fell ever deeper into debt. Both his wife and the Emperor demanded his presence in the capital so that he would be available to attend social and court functions, while he would much have preferred to be in the country, writing ('Worldweariness'). Though Nicholas gave him intermittent support socially and financially, many at court and in the government, wounded by his jibes or shocked by his supposed political and sexual liberalism, disliked or despised him. And a new generation of writers and readers were beginning to look on him as a man of the past.

In these years Pushkin wrote less; and when he did write he turned increasingly to prose. He developed his interest in history, already evident in *Boris Godunov* and *Poltava*: Nicholas I commissioned him to write a history of Peter the Great, but he only left copious notes for this at his death. He did, however, write in 1833 his *History of Pugachov*, a well-researched account of the eighteenth-century Cossack and peasant uprising under Yemelyán Pugachóv, which Nicholas allowed him to publish in 1834. He built on his research into this episode to write his longest work of prose fiction, the historical novel *The Captain's Daughter* (1836).

Other Writings From his school days till his death Pushkin composed 700 or more shorter verses, comprising, as well as love poems, many poetic epistles to friends, brief narratives, translations, pastiches, protests, invectives, epigrams, epitaphs, dedications and others. He left numerous letters from his adult years that give us an invaluable insight into his thoughts and activities and those of his contemporaries. And, as a man of keen intelligence and interest in literature, he produced throughout his career many articles and shorter notes – some published in his lifetime, others not – containing a wide variety of literary criticism and comment.

Death Early in 1837 Pushkin's career was cut tragically short. Following a series of improper advances to his wife and insults to himself, he felt obliged to fight a duel with a young Frenchman who was serving as an officer in the imperial horse guards in St Petersburg. Pushkin was fatally wounded in the stomach and died at his home in St Petersburg two days later. The authorities denied him a public funeral in the capital for fear of demonstrations, and he was buried privately at the Svyatýe Gory monastery near Mikháylovskoye, where his memorial has remained a place of popular pilgrimage.

– Roger Clarke

Select Bibliography

Books about Pushkin and His Work:
Tomashevsky, Boris Viktorovich, *Pushkin* (Moscow-Leningrad: Izdatelstvo Akademii Nauk USSR, 1956)
Bayley, John, *Pushkin: a Comparative Commentary* (Cambridge: Cambridge University Press, 1971)
Briggs, A.D.P., *Alexander Pushkin: a Critical Study* (London: Croom Helm, 1983)
Wolff, Tatiana, ed. and tr., *Pushkin on Literature* (London: The Athlone Press, 1986)
Lotman, Yury Mikhaylovich, *Pushkin* (St Petersburg: Iskusstvo-SPB, 1995)
Binyon, T.J., *Pushkin: a Biography* (London: HarperCollins, 2002)
Arinshtein, Leonid Matveyevich, *Pushkin: Neprichosannaya Biografiya* (Moscow: Rossiysky Fond Kultury, 2007)

Text of Pushkin's Lyrics and Commentaries in Russian:
Texts, with brief commentary, are available in numerous collections of Pushkin's works, published in the Soviet Union and in Russia during the last half-century and more, notably:
Sobraniye Sochineniy Pushkina, Vols. I–III (Moscow: Gosudarstvennoye Izdatelstvo Khudozhestvennoy Literatury, 1959–62). This ten-volume collection is also available online through the *Russkaya Virtualnaya Biblioteka* at www.rvb.ru/pushkin/toc.htm
Polnoye Sobraniye Sochineniy Pushkina v Dvukh Tomakh, Vol. I (Moscow: Izdatelsky Tsentr Klassika, 1999)
Polnoye Sobraniye Sochineniy Pushkina v Dvadtsati Tomakh, Vols. I and II (Book 1), containing lyrics from 1813 to 1820 (St Petersburg: Nauka, 1999–)

Pushkin's Lyrics: Translations into English:
The Complete Works of Alexander Pushkin in English Vols. I–III (Downham Market, UK: Milner and Company, 1999–2001)
Falen, James E., *Alexander Pushkin: Selected Lyric Poetry* (Evanston Illinois: Northwestern University Press, 2009)

Pushkin's Lyrics: Discussion and Commentaries in English:
Kahn, Andrew, *Pushkin's Lyric Intelligence* (Oxford: Oxford University Press, 2008)
Wachtel, Michael, *A Commentary to Pushkin's Lyric Poetry 1826–36* (Wisconsin: University of Wisconsin Press, 2011)

Index of Titles

Index of First Lines
in Russian (and English)

194

ALMA CLASSICS

ALMA CLASSICS aims to publish mainstream and lesser-known European classics in an innovative and striking way, while employing the highest editorial and production standards. By way of a unique approach the range offers much more, both visually and textually, than readers have come to expect from contemporary classics publishing.

～

To order any of our titles and for up-to-date information about our current and forthcoming publications, please visit our website on:

www.almaclassics.com